2.⁰⁰

UNCOMMON
SENSE

UNCOMMON SENSE

HOW TO DISCOVER THE PSYCHIC INSIDE YOU

PATRICIA EINSTEIN

VILLARD BOOKS NEW YORK 1989

Library of Congress Cataloging-in-Publication Data

Einstein, Patricia.
Uncommon sense.
1. Psychical research.   2. Success.   I. Title.
BF1031.E48   1989   133.8   88-40464
ISBN 0-394-57164-9

Book Design by Guenet Abraham

MANUFACTURED IN THE UNITED STATES OF AMERICA
9 8 7 6 5 4 3 2
FIRST EDITION

To anyone who's ever had a hunch or a flash of inspiration—and just went with it.

But, especially, to Peter

ACKNOWLEDGMENTS

SOMEWHERE IN THIS BOOK I NOTE that no mind is an island. Certainly, no book is either—leastwise this one. During the long process of putting together *Uncommon Sense,* so much help of all kinds came to me—sometimes from out of the blue—that I knew this book was somehow meant to be. It simply would have never come as fully into being without the inspiring aid of the following:

My teachers, who've included Louise L. Hay, Alexander Murray, and Phyllis Dahlby, each one providing both a loving beacon and an occasional cosmic kick along my path of growing awareness.

My students, who have been teachers all and have functioned in tandem as a living laboratory in preparation for this book; their responses to exercises they practiced in my workshops helped form the foundation of *Uncommon Sense*.

My colleagues, including David Tannenbaum, Christine Rakela, and Francisco Alameda, who, in contributing their professional two cents, have given me many times that worth in insight.

My darling husband, Peter, who became by default (as well as, I suspect, by choice), my twenty-four-hour-a-day author's inspiration and catalyst—a thankless task at times, yet one at which he clearly excelled; and the rest of my family and friends, too numerous to mention by name, each one of whom never ceased in giving me encouragement and advice whenever I needed it.

My organizational angels-in-disguise, including Kevin Jennings and Anthony Bruno, whose structural aid helped kick the project off; Aaron von Solos, whose many ideas helped keep it going; the incomparable aide-de-camp, Deborah Bergman, who gave so unstintingly of her expertise, lucidity, time, and even hardware; and Gila Sand, whose wordprocessing wizardry provided the perfect finish.

My beyond-the-call-of-duty agent, Christine Tomasino, who saw me all the way through *Uncommon Sense* and brought me and the book, happily, to Villard Books.

Special acknowledgment must go, of course, to the entire crackerjack staff at Villard, but especially to editor Diane Reverand and editorial assistant Emily Bestler, who each offered much more than merely brilliant editing assistance.

To each of the above, many thanks. You've blessed me all. Now go do your own books!

FOREWORD

As a professional psychic counselor and intuitive trainer, I've discovered something interesting. Although my clients and students come from many different walks of life and have many different points of view, they all find it easy to agree that there is such a thing as intuition.

Each of them, at one time or another, has had a certain

irrefutable, in-the-gut hunch. And many of them have also discovered the aha! of a flash of inspiration. However, not many have considered the origin of those experiences, or the possibility of willfully re-experiencing them.

That's where I come in. Over the years I've discovered that each of us has a psychic inside us, ever ready for us to tap its invaluable reservoir of inner knowledge. Possessing a seemingly endless supply of what I call *uncommon sense*, this resource exists within us all to provide deep insight, intuition, and creative inspiration to help guide us through virtually every area of our lives.

How exactly did I come to this conclusion? It seems I was always just as interested in the unseen elements of life as I was in what was seen as plainly as the nose on my face. I found it quite natural to study such disciplines as meditation and Eastern thought, both to absorb their mysteries and to increase my understanding of my everyday life. More and more, I came to perceive a new sort of logic that lay just beyond the bounds of what we are taught to accept as logical thought. It was every bit as vital and in many ways more valuable, if only it could be uncovered and used more readily.

One day, a friend mentioned a psychic development class that would be starting up soon and something struck a chord in me: Here was my passport within. Two weeks later, I was well on my way, unerringly guided on my voyage by the British psychic Phyllis Dahlby.

Phyllis was a natural teacher—an expert in giving people all the room they needed to grow while anchoring them to the real world at the same time. As she introduced each new exercise to our class, she would cheerfully but firmly intone in her irresistible accent, "And I don't want to hear the words *'I cahn't!'* " So it was first there I discovered that I could easily and consistently access this powerful inner logic, and, in fact, everyone could.

That first class led to the next, and to a network of other students who were also developing what I came to see as the psychic within. Each of my teachers taught me a special skill, had a unique way of reassuring me about my ability, and provided a new piece of the psychic puzzle. I even found key pieces to that puzzle in areas not generally considered psychic, as I integrated any new idea that seemed to add to my growing depth of understanding and overall developing philosophy. I started to realize that when I combined some very practical self-help concepts with the more intuitive abilities I'd been developing all along, the sky was really the limit.

Putting it all together, I came up with *Uncommon Sense.* The premise behind it is quite simple: Uncommon sense is not only everyone's inherent psychic awareness, but also a highly practical tool that can easily be applied to your daily life. I discovered that when you develop and tap into the vast spectrum of your uncommon sense, you learn how to tune into what's ahead for you and take an active part in shaping your own life events, as well.

Eventually, I found myself beginning to give my own psychic counseling sessions and developing my own uncommon sense workshops, both for individuals and corporations. Clients and students alike, from secretaries to artists to CEOs, started calling back to tell me how much the insight I'd given them had improved their lives. They also asked me to recommend books that would further their own ongoing voyage toward cultivating uncommon sense. They weren't alone—I, too, was on the lookout for a book that would both appeal to my interest in psychic matters and also offer practical, real-life guidance. I'd looked everywhere, but I could never find what I needed.

Then it dawned on me. Maybe the book was mine to write, so I could share all the wonderful knowledge and insight I'd been so lucky to gather over the years. Gradually, and much to my delight, this realization turned into the book you now hold in your hands.

So welcome to the world of *Uncommon Sense,* my take on the realm within. You'll find that this personal realm has little to do with your logical mind, but everything to do with your deepest personal knowledge. You probably won't become a psychic advisor once you gain this awareness—nor should you, unless your uncommon sense starts to tell you to. But it's my very strong hunch that you positively will notice a natural increase in the degree of creativity, success, love, and, of course, intuition you experience day by day.

The simple techniques presented in this book are the very same ones that professional psychics have used over the centuries to advise their clients on everything from business decisions, relationships, and finding lost objects to increasing personal creativity, productivity, love, and more. And they're just as entertaining as they are personally enriching.

Try them out. The more you practice them, the more

practical intuition and deeper insight will readily flow to you. You are sure to find the techniques very useful in your daily life. And I believe they will also reward and delight you for years to come, much as my own explorations have rewarded and delighted me. See how you, too, can discover that psychic inside you who's your surest, most reliable guide to the wonderful and rewarding world of uncommon sense.

—April 1989

CONTENTS

CONTENTS

CONTENTS

UNCOMMON
SENSE

YOUR INTRODUCTION TO UNCOMMON SENSE

Some people call it intuition. Some call it psychic ability—or the sixth sense. Some people know it as a flash of inspiration or a strong gut feeling, while others think of it as a little voice that whispers to them. Some feel it is perfectly normal and natural, and others think of it as something otherworldly. You may not believe in it at all, but despite your skepticism, you do have it. We all do. It's all part of what I call *uncommon sense.*

Uncommon sense is an inner awareness and a sense of knowing that is outside the realm of logical thought. Yet it possesses a wonderful flowing logic all its own. A powerful inner guide, uncommon sense manifests itself in the hunches and inspirations that lead you again and again to the added insight, new direction, creative breakthrough, or the ability to be in the right place at the right time. Yet its messages can also be so subtle you might not realize you're receiving them. You may be ignoring them altogether, or you may already simply accept them as a normal part of your everyday life—which is exactly what uncommon sense is.

Each day your uncommon sense can help guide you through everything from mundane matters—such as what to wear, where to find a parking space, or even what card to play—to important decisions, like who to share your life with, what career path to take, who to trust, and, in general, where to find the most fulfillment.

Just as developing your muscles through aerobics, calisthenics, and jogging is a way to physical fitness, developing your uncommon sense through the exercises described in this book is the way to inner fitness. As you develop your uncommon sense, you will find it a perfect complement to your everyday stock of commonsense logic. Uncommon sense will help you

- Know intuitively what your best choices are—and make them happen.

- Read between the lines and know what's going on behind the scenes at work and at home.

- Reap invaluable creative ideas from your dreams—and be more creative in real life than you ever dreamed of.

- Tune in to the right career moves and make the smartest business decisions.

- Meet your perfect mate—and truly know who's best for you.

- Be more in touch with the thoughts and feelings of friends, colleagues, and lovers—and improve any relationship.

- Respond to any situation with stronger convictions and a greater sense of confidence in your own inner knowledge.

- Experience the sheer joy of discovering and using a talent you never knew you had.

- And much, much more.

For some people, the whole concept of uncommon sense may seem a little farfetched. But the fact that you're reading this book indicates your readiness to explore your own inner abilities. Far from being exclusive to Indian yogis on mountaintops or eccentric grande dames in their parlors, uncommon sense is an inherent trait that we all have. Uncommon sense is not a rare gift; it is something that comes to everyone every day.

The telephone rings and you suddenly think of your old friend Joe. You answer it, and, lo and behold, it's Joe! That's uncommon sense.

You're dressing for work one morning when "something tells you" to dress a little better than you usually do, and you put on your best tie or blouse. Later that morning the boss calls you to an emergency client meeting. Aren't you glad you "listened" to that early morning hunch? That's uncommon sense.

You're sitting home reading a book one evening, but you just can't seem to concentrate on it. Somehow you can't stop thinking about your daughter who's away at college. For no apparent reason, you have a feeling that something isn't right with her. You call her at school and her roommate tells you she was admitted to the infirmary just that afternoon. Nothing too serious. But still—aha! That's uncommon sense.

In each of these cases, you were so in tune with a particular person or situation that pertinent, critical information just came to you. However, by expanding the realm of your intimate inner connections and by getting in tune with a larger source that connects *all* information, you can make uncommon sense work for you in almost every situation.

.　.　.

THE WHOLE BRAIN AND NOTHING BUT THE WHOLE BRAIN

Exactly how uncommon sense works is not known, though science has been working hard at finding out. In 1981, Roger Sperry won the Nobel Prize for his theory that the human brain is divided into two separate but equal hemispheres, each governing a different way of thinking. The left hemisphere houses logical, linear thought, and is characterized by objectivity, reason, analysis, criticism, and what is generally accepted as adult behavior. The right hemisphere is the home of intuitive, nonlinear thought, and is characterized by subjectivity, inspiration, play, creativity, childlike wonder, and psychic ability. Clearly the seat of uncommon sense is the right hemisphere of the brain.

Primitive man was probably much more right-brained in his thinking than we are today. His survival depended on his instincts and intuition. Tuning in to weather changes, geological shifts, and animal habits was crucial to him. He had to hunt for his food not only with all five senses, but with a keen sixth sense as well: his uncommon sense. It was uncommon sense that not only helped lead him to his dinner, but also told him to flee when he was in danger of becoming some other creature's meal.

As civilization progressed, humans became more left-brained in their thinking. Agricultural societies began to flourish, and the do-or-die awareness required by hunting was no longer crucial to survival. Thus man no longer had to depend on his instincts alone. Written language was devised to record knowledge, which meant that people ultimately came to feel more comfortable going by the book than they did living day to day guided by their uncommon sense as their cave ancestors had been doing.

Still, uncommon sense was never forgotten, and in many cultures it was revered. The ancient Greeks were the first great logical thinkers, yet they consulted the oracles for guidance. The leaders of ancient Rome, who prided themselves on ruling by reason and order, consulted soothsayers who read the entrails of animals for counsel. Shamans and seers still abound in many cultures around the world. And even in the late nineteenth century, famous American captains of industry like Andrew Carnegie, John D. Rockefeller, and Cornelius Vanderbilt regularly consulted psychics and largely ran their empires by intuition.

For the most part, history and science have discredited the achievements of uncommon sense with rational explanations. Today, in the information age, however, we are beginning to realize with a new clarity that the mind has access to information science alone cannot provide. Now that computers are doing so much of our left-brained thinking for us—collecting data, storing it, organizing it, and retrieving it on command—we are free to pursue more right-brained information. In fact, as computers take over more and more of our left-brain functions, our continued success—and survival—depends on developing the kind of thinking that computers *can't* do.

Nowhere is this more evident than in today's business world. Executives are now relying on their intuition to make business decisions, and studies have shown that those managers who merge intuition with logic consistently surpass their competitors in terms of sales and productivity. The Japanese, of course, pioneered the use of holistic thinking in business management, and their success is now legendary. After much resistance, American business and industry have begun to put their money where their uncommon sense is.

Obviously, the world has not completely converted to a right-brained point of view, and those who operate exclusively on the basis of their intuition are still looked upon with skepticism. Whenever I conduct corporate workshops and seminars, I deliberately avoid using the word *psychic* because of the negative connotations it has for some people. Yet what I teach these clients is very much the stuff of which psychics are made. My clients learn in essence what *I* learned: how to contact their innate intuition and creative problem-solving abilities.

In fact, there is an increasing demand in the corporate world for developing what is now being recognized as a basic skill, an uncommon sense logic that can augment the left-brained logic of analysis and data compilation. From the more creative businesses like advertising to the hard facts industries like high finance, professionals are using intuition to make better deals, improve management and people skills, and evolve their best ideas into fully realized projects.

STEP INTO MY OFFICE

As a psychic counselor, I look into my clients' lives in order to seek out and uncover any hidden meaning and direction. In so doing I guide them toward seeing themselves from an enlightened perspective so that they can live their lives and make decisions with more self-awareness.

As a private teacher and intuition trainer, I help people discover their own illuminating gifts. My students learn to tap into a never-ending source of information and to see their lives more clearly. In developing the psychic inside themselves, they begin to see beyond their preconceived notions of what it means to be psychic. I get tremendous satisfaction as I see the veil of mystery (and the fears that are often interwoven with it) lifting from their minds. What once seemed scary—due to spooky images conjured up by the media or perhaps a previous psychic experience that wasn't understood—is explained and experienced in a way that is open, natural, and far from threatening. My hopes are the same for you as you read this book.

FOR BEST RESULTS

As you continue to read, you will see that the exercises are highlighted and numbered. I suggest that you read through the entire book in the order it is written, doing the exercises as you go along. But if you happen to be drawn to any particular chapter, then go ahead and dip in with the understanding that the more accumulated information you have, the better you'll be at the exercises. By all means, jump to the sections on love or prosperity if that's what interests you, but accept them as a taste that will be more fully appreciated once you have given yourself the chance to digest the book in its entirety.

Once you've gotten the whole picture, you'll probably find that within that picture there are certain exercises you favor, and can see yourself having fun with. They *are* fun. By all means, share them with your friends. And keep the fun up.

The most important exercise for ongoing development of your uncommon sense is Exercise 17, "Balancing Your Energy with the Energy of Uncommon Sense." Try to do this one every day. It will help you get the best results from all the other exercises.

Although you can think of this as an inner fitness book, the goal is not to "go for the burn," as Jane Fonda puts it in her workout books. Instead, go for the *learn,* proceeding at your own pace, and stopping and starting as you wish. No one has more uncommon sense than anyone else. We're all involved in the ongoing process of developing our own connection to it, and practice makes perfect.

When you first begin to tune in to your uncommon sense, the information you receive may be subtle. Don't misconstrue it for failure and let yourself get discouraged.

If you keep practicing, the messages will come through—much stronger and clearer.

Remember this: The only thing you need to bring to the task of developing your uncommon sense is an open mind. Be willing to accept that it can be even more so. Back that up with your willpower to keep the mind-stretch going, and you're all set. Now get ready to discover your *own* wealth of guidance and information.

MAKING SENSE OF UNCOMMON SENSE

GOING WITH THE FLOW

Each of us has the ability to connect with more information than we realize, for each of us is already connected to a universal *source*—the source of all awareness. Think of the source as a bustling port on an ever-flowing river.

The river flows through every town and village, connecting each one to the port. So, too, we each are connected to our source—the source of all information—through what I call the *flow*. The flow is everyone's connection to an ever-flowing, ever-informing awareness.

But if each of us is already connected to this source, why don't we seem to have all the answers we need? In fact, we already have the answers we seek, but we often fail to connect with them. Simply put, our everyday awareness is usually not in line with the larger awareness, which is the source of uncommon sense. Like the river, uncommon sense is there for us, but to connect with the source, we've got to go with the flow.

Questions seem to pop up almost every day, and we need to connect with their answers. Another company has made you a great job offer, but you don't know if it's too good to be true, or too good to pass up. Or else, out of the blue you were handed your pink slip, and you haven't a clue what to do. Are you ever going to find Mr. or Ms. Right? Or have you already met him or her and don't even know it? Whatever the question, following the flow of your uncommon sense can easily help you navigate the uncertain seas of your life.

In recent years extensive studies have been conducted on the *flow state*, the state in which we sense the universal flow. Commonly associated with the peak performance of creativity, it is actually the state in which we seem to automatically make all the right moves, whether in thought or in action. In the flow state, the thoughts and feelings that in everyday life seem to get in the way suddenly disappear and are replaced by a flowing and powerful mental focus.

Everyone has experienced the flow state at one time or another while reading a good book, playing a particularly engrossing game of chess, or doing anything at all in which it's easy to get lost. It often feels like a state of euphoria during which everything falls into place, and solutions seem to flow to you naturally. How the flow state, which is rooted in the right brain, functions is unknown. Right now science can only tell us that it exists and that it *works*.

The first step in your quest for uncommon sense is to go with the flow, literally. As you enter the powerful flow state, your focus will begin to shift from everyday awareness, and open to a larger sense of knowing and understanding. In the flow state, you'll sense the interconnection of all information and experience, and from this state of awareness, you'll be able to draw rich nuggets of uncommon sense.

The flow connects all consciousness, all awareness, all information. Uncommon sense is its perfectly natural product. In essence, the flow state connects you with the source of all your answers. The following exercise will help you begin to get into the flow.

EXERCISE 1: FLOWING WITH THE FLOW

To immediately experience the flow, set aside some time—at least five minutes—to lie down and listen to flowing instrumental music. Don't listen to anything with lyrics because the words will distract you.

Let yourself float along with the music, not thinking about anything in particular, just allowing yourself to be carried with it. Don't try to force it. Just relax.

At the end of the piece, come back and take note of the difference between what you felt while the music was playing and what you feel now. Do you see a difference?

WHEN YOU'RE HOT, YOU'RE HOT

The flow state comes naturally during periods of intense concentration and creativity. Many musicians often seem to be lost in their music when they play. Think of the look of near rapture on Leonard Bernstein's face when he's conducting a symphony, or the totally into it expressions of rock guitarist Eric Clapton when he's leaning into a long, bluesy solo. Think of the keenly focused concentration on the face of Martina Navratilova during a tennis match. Rickey Henderson, the base-stealing star of the New York Yankees, says that when he's running the bases, his concentration is so intense he isn't even aware of his legs pumping or his feet hitting the ground. A leading outfielder has spoken of being "one with the ball" when he's "hot." When he knows what pitch is coming, he flows with it, literally *feeling* it come off the bat and, in what seems like the blink of an eye, "it's outta there." These people are at their peak and in the flow.

If you don't think you've ever been hot in the same way that a professional athlete or a world-class musician is, you're probably wrong. Most likely you've experienced the flow while making love! This particular flow experience is probably best left to the imagination, but suffice it to say that when you are caught up in the act of making love, you can experience intense concentration and pleasure to the point where nothing else, including time, exists.

In this state, you are definitely "on" and moving with the flow. Even the floating sensation experienced before, during, and directly after lovemaking is a part of that all-connecting flow. Try Exercise 3 to get in touch with your own natural flow, but first see if you can refresh your memory (and experience) with the help of Exercise 2.

EXERCISE 2: FLOW RECALL

Think of times when you've experienced a state of flow—making love, playing sports, playing music, dancing, painting, getting lost in your work or in a good book.

Next, focus on the experience and what you felt during that experience. Was it a sense of floating? Oneness? Deep tranquility or ease? Did you experience other unique sensations or a special, personal state of mind? Let the flow feelings engulf you, and hold on to them for as long as you can. Often we get dreamy when we're remembering a flow experience. Actually, this is just our natural, instinctive attempt to re-enter that flow.

If you have any trouble recalling the flow state, you may do better by recreating it from scratch. The following exercise will develop your control over the flow state so that you can get into it whenever you need it.

EXERCISE 3: CREATING THE FLOW

Take five minutes to let yourself go on paper or with a tape recorder. Doodle, draw, think out loud, anything at all, except don't think! Just float along with your stream of consciousness.

After five minutes, see what you have. You may be surprised to find that you have the germ of an idea, a better sense of your emotional state, a relaxing release of energy, or the groundwork for an idea to come as a result of this simple flow warm-up. Repeat this exercise before you start working on a project and whenever you get stuck on something in your work.

LEVELS OF AWARENESS

Everyone has had the experience of finally solving a difficult problem, once the problem has simply been let go. You may have started off by batting the problem around in your head until you felt like *it* was batting *you.* When there didn't seem to be any logical solution, you probably just got up and walked away from the darn thing in frustration and fatigue. Perhaps you actually got out of the house and took a walk to clear your head. Later, when you were relaxed and refreshed, you returned to this problem, and as if by magic, the answer just came to you! The solution may have been so obvious you couldn't quite believe it. "Why didn't I think of that before?" you asked yourself.

Well, the reason it didn't occur to you before is that you were actually *thinking* too much. When you stopped straining your left brain for a logical answer, you relaxed, got into the flow, and let the answer come to you through your own uncommon sense that connected you to a much larger awareness. This larger awareness or consciousness is vastly greater than the awareness any individual can tap from the left brain alone.

In fact, there are many different levels of awareness available to us through our uncommon sense, and many different ways of knowing things. While you were sweating it out trying to get the answer to your problem, you were just drawing on the limited funds of your left-brain bank of knowledge. But when you relaxed and got into the flow, you were drawing on the universal bank of *all* knowledge. The flow of this knowledge is the actual stream of consciousness—the greater awareness of uncommon sense.

Uncommon sense, then, is not the same as everyday awareness. It's a whole other state of mind. Yet, uncommon sense can be used every day.

Many Eastern philosophies, as well as the teachings of Don Juan, have likened this awareness to a warrior's state of mind at the height of battle. Highly aware of everything around him, he is also perfectly attuned to all that needs to be done, and exactly when. Who wouldn't want to face the day armed with that kind of mental ammunition?

In order to enter a state of peak awareness, one must first quiet the part of the mind that constantly categorizes and qualifies. The left hemisphere of the brain, in addition to being logical, is also sometimes maddeningly judgmental. An excess of intellectual judgment can lead to doubt and even squelch that powerful, instinctive spontaneity that keeps the warrior safe from harm. It's the part of the brain that wears the editor's and judge's hats and will keep on barking orders until you give yourself a break by allowing *it* to take one, too.

The next exercise is designed to help you give your left brain a break so that your right brain can be heard.

.   .   .

EXERCISE 4: TURNING OFF THE INTELLECT TO TURN ON INSIGHT

Lie down or sit in a straight-backed chair. Gently concentrating on your breath, begin to breathe deeply and rhythmically. Focus your attention on the very center of your forehead and breathe into this area, reinforcing your focus with each breath.

Notice how your focus becomes so strong that your thoughts slip away. If you catch yourself drifting off into evaluation or some other distracting mental activity (and you probably will), bring your attention back to that point in your forehead and keep on breathing into it rhythmically. You may also get ideas or insights in flashes. Make a note of these insights after you've come back. This is your entrance into a higher awareness, the beginning of your increasing uncommon sense.

Start with five minutes. When you feel comfortable with that time period, then go on as long as you like.

THE ONLY WAY TO KNOW IT IS TO KNOW IT

When you use your uncommon sense, you experience the answers it gives you very directly—you do not feel detached from the very situation you are considering. This means you cannot figure things out with uncommon sense. Instead, you simply allow the answers to come to you and in a very real sense allow yourself to become one with them.

When you use everyday reasoning, you follow a single, commonly accepted line of logic. However, when that sudden flash of knowing comes—knowledge that a certain person will call, a certain job will be yours, that a certain person is right for you, or that the perfect solution to a taxing problem has been reached—the line you follow is your own personally aligned connection to the larger logic of uncommon sense.

We must let the insight come whole, trying not to edit, question, or even intellectually understand it while it's being received. Later your intellect will read it back and register it in your consciousness as a definite piece of rational, practical information that can be applied to your daily life.

But insights, themselves, are not filtered through the constraints of logical understanding: They are not communicated through the vehicle of the left brain. Rather, they go directly to your experience, to your direct knowledge: territory that belongs to the right brain. It is here that we spontaneously see the whole picture, knowing and experiencing it at once.

Because our minds are normally so filled with intellectual, left-brain activity, at times we need to be "mindless" in order to avail ourselves of the larger awareness. A public relations director once told me she was a bit sorry that she didn't have to iron as much as she used to, because in the mindless monotony of performing that chore, she'd received a lot of unasked for, but gratefully received, inspiration. Here's an exercise to spark some inspiration of your own.

EXERCISE 5: AN EXERCISE IN MINDLESSNESS (TO JOG UNCOMMON SENSE)

This exercise is a perfect companion for running, swimming laps, using a rowing machine, taking a shower, doing housework, or mowing the lawn.

Before you start the activity, tell yourself that you are now open to your uncommon sense. Then, open yourself to the flow of the shower or the drone of the vacuum cleaner and "enter" it with your awareness, thinking or saying, "I'm opening to uncommon sense; insights and ideas are flowing to me now." Get into the rhythm of whatever you're doing and flow with it. You may be surprised at the insights that accompany so-called mindless activities.

■   ■   ■

TAKING A RIDE ON THE TIME/SPACE CONTINUUM

Atomic physics has changed our comprehension of time and space. But what modern scientists have only recently discovered, mystics have known for eons: All comprehension of space and time is only relative. Our understanding of time and space all depends on our state of mind or current circumstances. Everyone has experienced a moment when time seemed to stand still, and when space actually seemed to change in size—for example, when the walls seem to close in on you, or when your home is suddenly bigger because you are alone. Time flies when you're having fun, doesn't move at all when you're not. It's your *feelings* about the time or space you're experiencing that determine how you perceive them.

In the ever-present, ever-eternal flow of uncommon sense, there are no rigid delineations of space and time. It's all part of the same flow, the same continuous whole. When you enter the time/space continuum with the help of your uncommon sense, you will experience a sense of timeless time and spaceless space. When I psychically "see the future," I'm actually entering the continuum and reading the information that is there in its flow, which is the flow of *all* time. When you enter the flow, you, too, will sense it as a whole. You, too, will pick up information from *all* time, including, of course, the future.

We have all had sudden hunches at one time or another, irrefutable moments of insight. These are really the instantaneous results of dipping into the stream of the time/space continuum. When we do so, we shift out of our everyday sense of time, which is defined by a past, present, and future, and into timeless time, where we see a glimpse of the future as part of what it really is—*now*.

We enter the time/space continuum all the time in daily life with the help of our uncommon sense. An editor friend of mine had the experience of knowing something was up when the air at the office felt "heavy." Everyone seemed to sense an unhappy event was imminent, and indeed some of my friend's co-workers were soon laid off. Before I met my husband, I had recently moved to a new apartment. It was a perfectly fine place, but I sensed I wasn't going to be living there long and so I didn't do much decorating. Sure enough, I soon met my husband-to-be, moved to a much more spacious home, and began to decorate with a passion.

Remembering times in your life when you unwittingly sensed the inevitable will help you begin to read the future on a more conscious level.

EXERCISE 6: TIMELESS RECALL

Think of times you've had a feeling something was about to happen, or sensed an impending change. Perhaps you were playing cards and sensed that an ace was coming your way before you were actually dealt one, or perhaps you had a sudden inkling a friend, aunt, or cousin would be stopping by for a surprise visit just moments before the doorbell rang.

Maybe while working on a crucial business project you suddenly began to anticipate every unexpected development of the assignment before it came up, down to unanticipated reactions from your co-workers and superiors. Maybe you even dreamed about a key meeting, just to have your dream repeat itself in your waking life. Everything about your instincts was "on" and the difficult assignment seemed almost to complete itself!

Try to remember as many of these experiences as you can. Write them down. From now on, keep a log of new ones. You might want to refer to the Appendix for learning how to set up your own uncommon sense log. As you remember, try to recall just exactly what it was that made you "know" your hunch was irrefutable. Was it a gut feeling? Chills down your spine? An unshakable sense of elated glee? A quiet certainty? Whatever these feelings were, jot them down, too. You'll soon learn to quickly recognize the signals your uncommon sense is sending, and act on them with confidence.

. . .

THE STUFF DREAMS ARE MADE OF

Dreams are the best illustration of what you experience when you enter the time/space continuum. Dreams are rarely linear narrations. Events seem to happen outside of time, and one place may seem to be many places at once. The playground behind the grammar school you attended can simultaneously be the Roman Coliseum. Your brother can appear in a dream simultaneously as your brother—and Dan Rather! You may have a dream about your high school graduation when you are at your present age, your sister is a child, and Ulysses S. Grant is the school principal. While you're having the dream, all of this seems perfectly plausible.

It's only after you wake up and try to analyze the dream by imposing linear left-brain thinking on it that you realize the discrepancies in time and space. The experience of being in the time/space continuum is very similar to the experiences you have in dreams.

In fact, dreams can be a mother lode of uncommon sense information. Sometimes they seem prophetic; at other times they offer a running commentary on the issues you are working through in your life. In this sense they can provide direction and guidance, whether or not they provide prediction.

Some people do actually see the future in their dreams. Consider the case of my friend Aaron. When he was a child about to go to Europe with his family, Aaron dreamed about all the places they were going to visit.

When he eventually arrived, every church and side street, color, texture, and pattern turned out to be just as he had dreamed them.

Others, myself included, seem to see the future more often *outside* dreams. This does not make our dreams any less important. Perhaps you, too, through dreaming, have had the experience of getting a sense of what issues needed some looking into in your life. Or perhaps you received confirmation that certain approaches you'd taken to try to solve key problems were the right ones. For example, while working on this book I've had dreams that expressed the difficulty of putting all the elements together. Yet they were encouraging dreams, because they gave me the sense that I was indeed going to get through it.

EXERCISE 7: DREAM LOG

If you remember your dreams, start keeping a record of them. Try not to edit or interpret them. As we discussed earlier, the time/space continuum of dreams is often not logical. So keep track of what you remember and see if any patterns come up.

Are you more often indoors or outdoors in your dreams? Are you in any particular place? Does it seem that you're always on some kind of journey? Do certain feelings seem to come up again and again? Do events actually take place after you've dreamed them? Do you see any kind of message in the pattern?

Later on, we'll discuss how to interpret your dreams. But for now, just keep a record of what comes up and see for yourself what you get out of it.

TIME IS ON YOUR SIDE

Psychologist and author Lawrence LeShan calls our experiences in the time/space continuum "clairvoyant reality." Our everyday awareness he calls "sensory reality." Our sensory concept of time is composed of a past leading to a present, which in turn leads to a future. This way of thinking, he says, can interfere with the free flow of information. To get to the unlimited bounty of uncommon sense, we must transcend the bounds of sensory reality, enter the flow of timeless time, and become a channel for its information.

It's not difficult to discover your own inherent ability to channel timeless time. By dipping into the flow of clairvoyant time, you will learn to disregard the constraints of time as it is commonly understood, and become your *own* timepiece.

. . .

EXERCISE 8: TIME AWARENESS

Try to determine what time it is by visualizing the large white face of a clock and seeing the position of the hands. Tune in to the physical details of the clock. Are the hands black? Are the numerals Roman? If the clock were a pie, how big would the slice formed by the hands be? The more detailed your vision of the clock can be, the more informed your guess will be. Check your time against a real clock.

The best time of day to try this is right after you wake up in the morning. If you always wake up at the same time, try it on the weekends when you're not on your regular schedule. You'll be amazed at how close you can come to the actual time, and with practice you'll get better. By doing this, you'll be overcoming your reliance on the sensory concept of time, while also literally eliminating the need to be a "clock watcher."

As you continue with my program for developing uncommon sense, you will find you also have an ability to see future time in much the same way you have just seen present time. The only difference is that when you're ready to start sensing future time, you'll be looking for the position of the hands of time on the blank face of the *eternal* now.

HERE, THERE, AND EVERYWHERE

Geographical distances do not weaken your awareness of clairvoyant reality. Not only is all time "now" in the time/space continuum, but all space is "here," too, without any of the barriers that are part of our sensory reality.

In clairvoyant reality, here is there, there is here, and here is everywhere. Therefore, in the realm of uncommon sense it's not unusual to get a strong, accurate feeling about someone who is geographically quite far away.

Actress Kathleen Noone, one of the leading ladies of the daytime soap *All My Children,* told me a harrowing tale about an all-consuming apprehension she once had concerning her sister, who was off skiing in Colorado. Later she discovered that at the very time she was feeling apprehensive, her sister, who had been caught in an avalanche, was fighting for her life. Fortunately, Kathleen's sister survived. But it's significant that Kathleen was able to feel her beloved sister's distress so many miles away. That apprehension came to her through the flow of uncommon sense.

An antiques dealer friend came upon a deal that seemed too good to pass up. It was a guaranteed original Ming vase, going for a song, and it looked real enough to his trained eye, but an inner voice told him loudly to move on. Sure enough, the vase turned out to be just about as Chinese, let alone Ming, as his Irish grandmother, and nowhere near as old!

In case you're wondering why the sudden distant call

of uncommon sense frequently concerns a deeply emotional situation, there's a simple explanation. Emotions are a right-brain function. The more powerful our feelings are, the more completely they can overcome the strictly rational gatekeepers of our left brain. When those natural intuition barriers are flooded out by our deep feelings, our intellectual back talk gets drowned out, and uncommon sense messages can come through loud and clear.

GETTING IN SYNCH

We've all had the experience of being in the right place at the right time, and at some point in our lives we've all known someone who we characterized as lucky. Luck, however, is not a matter of chance. It's really a question of *synchronicity.*

The renowned psychologist C. G. Jung defined synchronicity as "meaningful coincidence." You might describe it as a string of events that seem to come from out of the blue but in fact happen for a reason. Because the reason cannot be explained in any rational, linear fashion, we tend to attribute it to chance.

Synchronicity is the process of getting in line with a larger awareness. Suddenly you seem to be in synch with the fates. We experience the synchronicity of meaningful coincidence all the time. It's that all-so-common occurrence of thinking of John and then running into him, or hearing from Jane out of the blue after you'd just brought her name up in a conversation. It's there again when certain words or numbers pop up with increasing regularity and no apparent reason until you finally decide they might have some kind of deeper message for you.

For example, a model friend of mine kept hearing about Japan and saw references to that country everywhere. Finally, he realized he was meant to go there. His trip was a very successful one and laid a real foundation for his entire career. Some might say he just got lucky, but getting lucky in and of itself is really the process of tuning in to your own synchronicity.

Sometimes you can even unconsciously make something happen just by getting in synch with what you want. You don't always have to follow signs like my model friend did to reap the benefits of synchronicity. Sure, you can start listing the symbols that have personal meaning for you, jotting them down when they come up. There will be much more about this process, which I call using your uncommon sense log, throughout this book.

But just deciding very clearly what it is that you want will allow that desire to reach the larger you. That larger, unconscious you in turn taps into the even larger awareness of synchronicity, and soon that giant information bank will send what you desire your way.

Not only can you enlist the assistance of the larger awareness in helping you achieve your own goals and fulfilling your personal needs, but you can also synch *yourself* with what's going on around you, beginning to make the choices in your life that are most in tune with you and with the flow. Once you've begun developing your natural synchronicity (the following exercises will help do the trick) you'll find yourself the grateful recipient of what many call good timing and lucky coincidences. But you'll know that you've merely gotten in synch with the flow to make the most appropriate (dare we say, in-tune?) choices for your own future.

Here's an example of what I'm talking about. A client of mine in advertising opened to his own synchronicity instinctively, with great results. From the minute he heard about it, he knew he had to have a DeLorean sports car. He started collecting any article and promotional material he could find, and it began to seem that wherever he looked, the DeLorean was mentioned.

Fueled with his own hunch and the many seeming coincidences, my client even went so far as to put down a deposit on a car, sight unseen, long before the first DeLorean was off the assembly line. Many months later, when the DeLorean account was up for grabs and every major ad agency was vying for it, the small firm he worked for won the plum account. Part of the coup had to do with showing off my client's contract in their winning presentation—more synchronicity.

But even that wasn't the end of it. Eventually, my client got to drive DeLorean's own car, and went on to write the prophetic line, "Live the dream"—which more or less described what had happened in his own life once he got himself in line with his most exciting possibility. In fact his life exceeded the dream, because flowing with his desire at the right synched time also wound up enhancing his professional reputation. You, too, can learn to recognize and plumb the hidden riches of the meaningful coincidences in your life.

EXERCISE 9: SYNCH RECALL

Think back and try to remember when you've experienced meaningful coincidences: instances when you happened to tune into someone you were thinking about, when a chance meeting led to your getting something you really wanted, or when you felt you were extraordinarily lucky. Also recall times when you felt you were in perfect synch with your surroundings: getting to the train station just as your train arrived, finding a parking space right in front of the store, being the very first to learn of a job opening. Write down these experiences, and keep a log of future meaningful coincidences.

I'VE BEEN HERE BEFORE

Déjà vu is a form of synchronicity. That strong yet inexplicable feeling that you've been here before is a meaningful coincidence that stems from the fact that you *have* been there before—but not in the sensory realm of everyday reality. In the larger awareness of clairvoyant reality you are able to be virtually everywhere in space and time. In the clairvoyant realm of uncommon sense it makes perfect sense to feel as if you have, indeed, been there before. When you experience déjà vu, some event, some person, some object is spurring you to recall just a fragment of all you know through your innate connection to other realities.

You can use déjà vu to come out on top in everyday situations. A lawyer I know was having apprehensions about a very important upcoming meeting. When I helped him to get in touch with his uncommon sense, we found he had what he called a "vision" of how the meeting would go. This vision was very detailed. It included what everyone would be wearing and saying—including himself—and ended in a very favorable outcome for my client. When the meeting actually took place it went exactly the way he'd envisioned it. It was déjà vu. As a result, this lawyer was able to do exactly what he needed to do to get the result he wanted in a highly charged situation. With the help of synchronicity—and déjà vu in particular—my client was able to create his own good fortune.

A computer salesman I know who works for an aggressive start-up company had a similar experience. Everybody in the company was chewing their fingernails down to the bone, worrying about an upcoming meeting with their biggest prospective client to date. But my friend was the only one who wasn't worried. That was because he'd already gotten a "flash" of the client with a big smile on his face. When the meeting finally came to pass, the client was ready to sign on the dotted line, and did so grinning from ear to ear. My friend wasn't surprised, though, because his uncommon sense had already shown him what the client's attitude would be.

THAT SYNCHING FEELING

Good game players and successful gamblers are prime examples of people aligning with their synchronicity. The newspapers are filled with stories of lottery winners who felt the luck of certain numbers, and kept on playing them until they hit the jackpot. My housekeeper did very well betting on numbers that came to her through the synchronicity of her dreams. And the recent winner of a national poker championship said she felt lucky that day and knew she would be dealt the winning hand.

Those who are good with investments—from penny stocks to megabuck mergers—are also allowing the aligning forces of synchronicity to inform and guide them. A real estate investor told me he'd just happened upon an article about a man who he sensed would be the perfect partner in a deal he had in mind. They met, seemed to synch with each other, and are now involved in a profitable multimillion dollar property.

It's important to practice making synchronicity work for you. The next two exercises should prove challenging. Remember, like the old joke about getting to Carnegie Hall, it takes practice, practice, practice. By simply repeating these exercises you'll be toning down the noise of your intellectual backtalk and turning up the sweet music of your own uncommon sense.

EXERCISE 10: INCREASING THAT SYNCHING FEELING, PART I—EVERYDAY PREDICTIONS

Try guessing at things before they happen: when the telephone will ring, who'll be at the other end of the phone line once you pick up, when a traffic light will turn green. Try to pick the winners at a horse race. While watching a TV game show, try to answer the questions before the contestants do and see how good you are at synching with the correct answers.

EXERCISE 11: INCREASING THAT SYNCHING FEELING, PART II—THE CARD TRICK

Choose a regular playing deck or make your own cards. For the playing deck technique, take a regular deck of cards. Put it face down. Predict what the first card will be, and turn it over. Start off easy, predicting only whether it will be a black or red card. When you're ready, graduate to suits. As your proficiency increases, try guessing individual cards, but make it easier on yourself by playing the intuitive odds. Is the number on the card higher than five? Lower than ten? Is it a royal card or a numbered card?

Creating your own cards approximates the actual tests performed by psychic researchers. Cut paper into pieces of the same size (cutting a few pieces of fairly heavy eight-by-ten-inch paper into quarters works fine). Then, with heavy felt pens in primary colors (red, yellow, blue, and also green) draw symbols on those cards (e.g., a circle, a triangle, a star, and a square). Follow the playing deck exercise, except this time guess first what color you have. Then guess which symbol is on the same card. Once you get the hang of it, try to hit the exact color and symbol.

Of course, the more precisely you try to pinpoint the cards, the more difficult the exercise will be. Keep on trying, though (at the pace and level that feel right to you), and don't be discouraged. As I said, repetition greatly improves your ability. At the same time, these exercises work on your psychic muscle, developing your ability to open to uncommon sense in your daily life. Keep on practicing! Once you start to click with the exercises, you'll be amazed at your own abilities.

A footnote to the synching exercises: As you practice both of these exercises, notice how you feel when you're "on" and "in synch." Do you pick up signals from your body—a feeling in your gut or a tingle at the back of your neck or up your spine? Other senses can be involved. A songwriter once told me his songs "smelled good" when they were "on." Other people may feel a slight ringing in the ears or seem to actually hear the answer they seek.

Anything that feels right will express itself through the best and strongest form of communication for you. I personally get a sense of balance versus imbalance—a sense that all the right information seems to fit. Sometimes you just "know." Remember what this experience feels like for *you*, and try to apply it to your exercises to see if you can determine what's merely a guess, what seems like a hunch, and what's a beyond-any-doubt sure sense of a perfectly nailed answer.

MIND SHAPES MATTER, OR MINDING YOUR OWN REALITY

To access uncommon sense, it's crucial that you be open both to the reality of its existence and to the certainty that you can make use of it in your life. In fact, you can't perceive what you don't believe. Simply put, the journey to uncommon sense starts with an open mind.

Nobody reading this book is expected to have the over-whelming belief of a saint, but by maintaining an open mind, having the will to start developing yours, and being willing to believe, you will find uncommon sense beginning to flow through, effectively developing a belief and faith in that reality.

In order to truly open to the larger wealth of uncommon sense and bring home its goodies, we must begin to examine the system of our own beliefs and cast off the limiting concepts that can block the whole picture of uncommon sense information.

EXERCISE 12: BELIEF SYSTEM REVIEW

Examine your attitudes about yourself. Has your belief in what's possible determined what has actually happened to you in your life? Can you think of other people whose negative or positive attitudes have determined events in their lives? For example, in every crowd there seems to be one pessimist who walks around with a dark cloud over his or her head. Indeed, disaster seems to be just around any corner this sad sack is near. Likewise, everyone knows a cockeyed optimist whose Pollyanna attitude seems too good to be true, and yet seems to always pull out a plum whenever he or she sticks a finger into any pie.

A MIND IS A TERRIBLE THING TO CLOSE

A young woman once came to me for a reading, desperately seeking a solution to her career dilemma. She was a not-very-successful success systems developer who ran seminars to help business people excel in their careers. This struck me as rather ironic considering her own terribly negative personality. I knew that before she'd ever be successful in her field we'd have to do something about her gloomy attitude. So I asked her to think back and recall something she really wanted and eventually got—a sweater, a ring, a car, anything at all. She couldn't think of a single thing. "Anything at all?" I persisted. She just frowned and shook her head. "Even a popsicle?" I said. "I hate popsicles!" she exploded.

As we proceeded into the reading, I realized this client's overwhelming negativism choked not only the flow of *her* uncommon sense, but also severely diminished the amount of information I could obtain for her. Her closed-minded attitude about life in general prevented her from making any positive—let alone intuitive—moves. As a result, her negativity was reinforced even further.

I sensed, however, that as a child there had been a time when she felt open to positive possibilities. I asked her to tune in to that time and hold every detail of that memory in her mind. At first she frowned, but eventually began to recall a glorious week on her grandparents' farm. So many delightful, unexpected things had happened: She'd

watched a litter of puppies being born, joined a spontaneous moonlit hayride, and had a gorgeous butterfly light
and then linger on her hand. As she relived the experience, she could feel herself confidently awaiting the *next*
wonderful event. "Hold on to that feeling!" I cried. Because that was precisely the open, trusting state she
needed to be in to start re-experiencing wonderful things
from then on.

So I advised her to regularly recall that scene, especially
the positive feeling she'd had about herself and her future,
and realize that she was, in fact, the same confident girl.
At first she felt a little doubtful, but about a month later
I received a call thanking me for the advice. "Would you
believe," she laughed, "I kept remembering the farm just
because it felt good, but my next seminar was actually a
success!"

OPENING THE MIND—TO CROSS THE BRIDGE

The mind's openness to uncommon sense allows it to
bridge the gap between the logic of everyday reality and
the alternate logic of uncommon sense. This other logic
is really just an extension and a complement to what we
are already aware of. Uncommon sense not only makes
invaluable information yours for the taking, but also can
effect actual physical transformation. The mind's openness combined with an individual's will to not only re-

ceive but also project uncommon sense has been known to produce spectacular results.

Faith healer Olga Worrel can change the molecular composition of water, actually converting its weight through simple willpower. Instances of psychic healing and psychokinesis (telepathic movement of objects) have been well documented. In parapsychological tests, it has been proven that people will score more psychic "hits" by wishing or willing the outcome. Furthermore, the ability of the mind to change matter has also stood up to the scrutiny of hard science. Research into quantum physics has proven that the subatomic world moves in actual relationship to the thoughts of those observing it. In other words, the reality of what we observe is actually being shaped by our own minds.

The following exercise is a real mind bender. It demonstrates how your thoughts can literally reshape physical reality. Although it may seem to be quite advanced, it is actually simpler than it sounds. The important thing to remember here is patience. Don't rush through any of the steps, and if you don't succeed at first, give yourself time to get it.

A client of mine got it so well he decided to lead his entire office in a mind-bending jamboree. Everyone grabbed the nearest suitable object, with letter openers responding so well that by the end of the week there were no unbent specimens to be found in the whole office. Go slowly through the instructions, visualizing all the way, and be willing to accept your own power.

EXERCISE 13: SPOON BENDING—AN EXERCISE IN MIND OVER MATTER

Find an inexpensive cafeteria-quality spoon and test its resistance to make sure it's not so flimsy that you can bend it yourself with little effort. (Please note: A piece of heavy silverware may be too tough for a beginner to bend, and if you do manage to bend the good family silver, you probably won't be able to bend it back into its exact original shape.)

Using both your hands, hold the spoon out horizontally in front of you in both hands. Hold one end of the spoon inside each fist with the curve in the handle pointing up. Close your eyes and start breathing rhythmically.

Now concentrate and visualize a ball of bright white light over your head. Concentrate as hard as you can on getting the light bright and hot as you move it down through the top of your head.

Once it's in your head, keep concentrating on it until you feel it is as bright as it can be. Then, slowly visualize the ball moving down your neck, into your shoulders, down your upper arms, down your forearms, and finally into your wrists. Focus only on the light and feel the energy of it vibrate as it warms you.

When the light reaches your fingers, say out

loud, "Bend, bend, bend!" and try to bend the spoon in one quick motion. Amazingly, the spoon will bend in the middle, as if it were suddenly made of butter, with almost no effort at all.

EVERYTHING IS ENERGY

W̲ITH HIS FAMOUS EQUATION E = mc², Albert Einstein proved that when you come right down to it, everything in the universe is energy. Both the physical reality of matter and the abstract reality of the mind are made up of patterns of energy. Connecting with your uncommon sense is the act of tuning in to the never-ending flow of universal energy.

The concept of a universal energy flow is not a new

one. The ancient Chinese called this flow *chi;* the ancient Hindus called it *prana.* The disciplines that developed in those two cultures—t'ai chi and yoga, respectively—are based on the art of tuning in to the flow of energy and using it to center the self. When we are centered, we experience harmony—not only with ourselves, but with others, and with our entire environment. Any centering process is actually the act of balancing ourselves with the universal flow of energy.

WHAT'S THE FREQUENCY?

Like other electromagnetic frequencies including X rays, radio waves, and light waves, the psychic flow is also an ongoing current of energy. In a sense, tuning in to uncommon sense is like tuning in to a station on the radio. When we tune in, we're literally on the same wavelength of any frequency we desire.

Just as many light waves on the color spectrum are invisible to the eye, the frequencies of uncommon sense are undetectable to those who are not specifically tuned in to them. But the more sensitive we become to their energy, the more we are able to tap into uncommon sense. In fact, the term, *sensitive,* which is often associated with psychics, was originally used to describe people who could detect the energy surrounding magnets and other objects.

Science has proven that there is an identifiable field of

electromagnetic energy surrounding each of us. Through a special process known as Kirlian photography, this field becomes visible to the naked eye. Kirlian photographs of humans, plants, and even certain inanimate objects show an aura emanating from each one. This field of energy, which surrounds us all, stems from the larger universal energy field, the flow. We all conduct the energy of the flow, and degrees of this energy naturally radiate throughout each one of us.

STAR LIGHT, STAR BRIGHT

Pregnant women are said to glow. Brides are radiant. Saints are traditionally portrayed with bright halos around their heads. Those whose talent has earned them fame and fortune seem to possess an extra helping of charisma and are known as stars. When a person makes a big breakthrough in his or her understanding of life, we say that person has finally seen the light.

It's no coincidence that when people are in states of high energy they are described in terms of increased light. Light is the palpable expression of energy, which in turn composes all reality. In this sense, we are all children of light, and everybody truly is a star.

You need not bother with expensive Kirlian photographs to prove that you emanate this light flow yourself. The following exercise will demonstrate the energy that you yourself radiate.

EXERCISE 14: FEELING YOUR ENERGY FIELD

Briskly rub your hands together, working up the warmth. As soon as they feel good and toasty (this only takes about thirty seconds or so), hold your hands palm to palm, lining up the fingers.

Now slowly begin to pull your hands away from each other again until you feel a push or a pull (some people feel one, some feel the other) that seems to suggest you've come to the outer edge of a chunk, or field, of energy. Usually this occurs when your hands are four to eight inches apart.

If you don't get it the first time keep trying the exercise again until the sensation occurs. I promise you it will. Some people don't feel the edge until they actually play with the field itself, moving their hands closer together and then farther away as if playing cat's cradle with a marshmallow. Try this yourself. Once you get the push/pull going between your hands, you'll get the idea of what the energy field feels like and how to sense it more easily.

The energy field you sensed between your hands is actually your own aura, the palpable, radiant energy that surrounds you. You have just learned to sense one part of your aura's boundary. In the next exercise, you'll learn to explore the parameters of a partner's energy field.

EXERCISE 15: SENSING THE BODY'S ENERGY FIELD

Find a partner and sit down with him or her in a pair of straight-backed chairs. In this exercise you and your partner will take turns being the subject and the sensor.

The subject must close his or her eyes and begin to breathe deeply and rhythmically. Meantime, the sensor should warm up with Exercise 14. When you're both feeling properly relaxed, the sensor must stand behind the subject, who is still seated, and raise his or her hands until they are about a foot above the partner's head.

Very slowly move the hands down until, as in the previous exercise, the sensor starts to feel the shift in energy that marks the literal edge of the subject's aura. Again, the sensor can play with that squishy-feeling energy flow until he or she feels exactly where the demarcation lies.

The perimeter of each individual's personal energy field varies widely, and some people have much more prominent and more easily sensed auras than others. So if you don't feel

anything, don't worry about it—just try again.
You can always move on and come back to it
later when you feel more energetically charged.

When you're ready, switch roles and repeat
the process.

You've already felt your own aura, but this next exercise
will show you your own visible light connection to the
energy flow of life.

EXERCISE 16: SEEING THE ENERGY FIELD

Find a black or very dark surface in your home
(a piece of clothing, a tabletop, or even a
turned-off television). Turn off any electric
lights, pull the shades, and place a single lighted
candle behind you.

Put your hands in front of the black surface
and examine them. You should see a whitish,
filmy glow emanating from your fingers. Try
this with a friend and experiment with the
filmy shadows. See how close you have to come
for your mutual films to touch.

This is what is truly meant by "Reach out and
touch someone!" When we feel touched without any physical contact, we are actually experiencing shared energy. When we say a person
has an aura of mystery or an aura of contentment, what we are really saying is that we have

sensed that person's energy field, and are inter-preting what that radiating energy represents.

The physical aura is not always easy to see because it can be very subtle. Don't be dis-couraged, though. When you do begin to see your glow, try increasing it through concentra-tion. Wishing and concentrating will project energy, and you'll see the auric field more clearly.

THE ENERGY LINEUP

Now that you've learned to see and feel your own energy field, it's time to get down to the fine points—the very specific *points* of energy that line up to form the internal energy system of your entire aura.

Our own energy field is composed of seven major en-ergy centers, each of which is associated with a different key location within the body. Each of the seven centers contributes a different essential quality to the internal energy flow. And just as white light can be separated into many colors when filtered through a prism, the bodily energy spectrum breaks down into individual hues.

Understanding these individual energy centers, their corresponding colors and how they all interrelate as a whole, remote as it may seem, really helps us to better understand—and make better use of—the whole system of uncommon sense. The more sensitive you become to different colors and the different energies they represent, the more sensitive you'll become to *all* the energy around you. As you develop your uncommon sense, you may very well start receiving information in the form of colors, so keep the following list in mind, or within close reach. For more specific data on uncommon uses and interpretations of color, you can also refer to Chapter 5 and the Appendix.

THE FIRST ENERGY CENTER: RED. Located right at the base of the spine, the domain of the first energy center also includes the reproductive region. This entire area is governed by the color red. No wonder we most associate red with raw passion and emotion, physicality, vitality, and sexuality!

Think of the hot sports car that's always advertised in red to get you lusting after it, or the shiny red apple a day that keeps the doctor away.

THE SECOND ENERGY CENTER: ORANGE. Moving up a little from the base of the spine and slightly to the left, you'll find the spleen, which is represented by the warming color of orange. The essential qualities here are wisdom, confidence, courage, and strength.

Think of the rich, tawny mane that crowns the strong—and, of course, courageous—lion.

THE THIRD ENERGY CENTER: YELLOW/GOLD. The third energy center is located at the solar plexus right at the center of the body—directly under the breastbone and spilling into the area we commonly refer to as the gut. It's no coincidence, then, that the saying "to know something in your gut" means to know something so deeply and surely that you feel it at your very core—or literal physical center.

The third center's governing color, yellow, is associated with intellect, self-awareness, knowledge, and personal power. Why do you suppose that the typical pencil or legal pad is most often colored yellow? The intellectual sharpening effects of yellow make it a perfect choice.

THE FOURTH ENERGY CENTER: GREEN/PINK. From the gut, we move up to the heart: the fourth energy center and the literal heart of the energy lineup. The heart's governing colors are green and pink. Green represents growth— both physical and emotional—and love and prosperity.

Think of the green shoots and buds that are the first lovely signs of a new spring. Then think of the very real color of money—the literal green of cash.

The pink hues associated with the heart symbolize the more tender, sweetening aspects of love. Maybe that's why the expression "in the pink" so succinctly expresses the sweet picture of perfection.

THE FIFTH ENERGY CENTER: BLUE. At the throat is the fifth energy center that governs both the flow of creative expression and the calm flow of tranquility.

Blue is the color that represents the energy of this center, and it all makes perfect sense when you think of how peaceful and rejuvenated you feel when you gaze at the ocean or the sky.

THE SIXTH ENERGY CENTER: VIOLET. Smack in the middle of the forehead is where we find the well-known third eye—the sixth energy center and the by-now clichéd but very real passageway to spiritual awareness. Its governing hue is violet. Together, this point and color represent our ability to achieve the highest, most divine knowledge.

Purple has always been the symbol of high endeavors and high connections. Think of the purple robes of kings and religious figures.

THE SEVENTH ENERGY CENTER: WHITE. This point, the seventh energy center, also known as the "crown chakra," is located at the very top of the head and represents our true crowning glory. Its governing color, white, quite naturally caps the entire energy lineup, as it's the radiant hue we most closely associate with the aura. Just think of all those artistic renderings of a glowing halo crowning the head.

White also represents purity, enlightenment, and protection. Think of the quintessentially pure image of a bride in her cascading white veil, or the angel that crowns a Christmas tree.

Whenever you feel you might need a "shot" of some enlightening energy and even extra protection, try visualizing a white light surrounding you or your environment. This is an ancient trick that really cuts through negativity and is perfectly helpful—and sometimes essential—in everyday modern life!

LINING UP THE LINEUP

When we are feeling at our best, the seven energy centers within each of us are lined up one by one to help create a sense of personal harmony, as well as a growing awareness of harmony with the universal energy flow of uncommon sense.

The more literally together our energy is, the more at ease we feel with ourselves, and the more smoothly we're able to get in synch with the larger awareness of uncommon sense. Just as we wake up in the morning and stretch first thing to get the energy flowing and readjust the body after a night's sleep, we can also add a daily stretch for the body's energy centers to realign ourselves and reawaken our connection with the flow itself.

The exercise that follows is *key* to opening to uncommon sense on a daily basis. Every morning I follow this simple routine of energy alignment. Try it to experience the same benefits yourself. I'm thoroughly convinced that this routine will open you to greater uncommon sense as well as a greater sense of general well-being. My students have all reported back with marvelous results.

It's most important that you master this exercise to develop your connection to uncommon sense. By all means, go on with the book. But please remember this is *the basic exercise* for everyday ongoing development. The more you practice alignment, the more quickly your own uncommon sense will get into line with the larger awareness.

EXERCISE 17: BALANCING YOUR ENERGY WITH THE ENERGY OF UNCOMMON SENSE

Find a quiet place where you won't be distracted, and either lie down or sit securely in a straight-backed chair. Start to breathe rhythmically and deeply. Take all the time you need to feel really comfortable and to let your breath flow easily and regularly.

When you feel perfectly comfortable, bring your awareness to the middle of your forehead and visualize a violet light at this point. Using your breath, release and relax into your awareness of this point, and see the light there. The violet light can seem to have a circular form, or perhaps it suffuses your entire third eye area with its glow. Use whatever works for you, breathing into your awareness. Stay there for a little while, perhaps a minute or more.

Next shift your awareness to the center of your throat area, remembering to continue your deep, relaxed breathing. Breathe into the throat area, and visualize a blue light there. Stay with that blue light for a while, until the light is very clear for you.

Move on to your heart area (in the middle of your chest) and visualize a green light there as you breathe and relax into your awareness of this essential area. Take your time; don't rush. Really enjoy this special time for renewing and refreshing your connection with the awareness of uncommon sense.

When you're ready, move on to the solar plexus. The solar plexus is the point under your breastbone that moves in and out when you breathe deeply, as you are doing now. As you breathe into the solar plexus area, see a golden yellow light suffusing the entire area with its glow. Stay with your breathing and your awareness for as long as it's comfortable for you to do so, really seeing and feeling that golden light.

Then find your spleen (it's on the left side of your body toward the back, near your kidneys). Breathe through this area as you visualize an orange light bathing it in its glow. There may be warmth, or another feeling associated with this color.

Finally, shift your awareness down to the very bottom of your spine, and visualize a red light there, heating the entire area with its radiant glow. Breathe and release into this red light as long as you like.

Now imagine a crystalline tube running downward from the base of your spine to the center of the earth. Feel and see a crystalline light in the center of the earth that is at once healing, releasing, and balancing. Now sense that light moving up through the crystalline tube, entering your body through the base of your spine, and working its way up through all the vertebrae and energy centers: healing, cleaning, releasing, and balancing you and your energy.

Feel and see the light move up through each energy center, moving up and out through the top of your head. Now feel and see this light as a crystalline lightning rod connecting you with the flow of infinite energy, the source of all uncommon sense.

Try this next variation whenever you feel you need to strengthen your uncommon sense connection.

EXERCISE 18: CONNECTING TO THE UNIVERSAL FLOW

Lie down or sit up straight in your quiet place and do the energy-balancing exercise (number

17), breathing through the energy centers as you visualize the various colored lights. When the crystalline light begins to beam out from the top of your head like a lightning rod, think or say out loud, "I now connect to the never-ending flow of all energy, all awareness." Keep breathing into the middle of your forehead as you repeat the phrase, and continue to flow with the energy of that crystalline light.

NO MIND IS AN ISLAND

Although your mind is just one small part of the energy of all existence, it contains the totality of all energy, all information: It is a universe in itself. In addition, your mind is already connected with and reflects the other universes of other minds. What that means in everyday terms is that your own thinking has already absorbed the thinking of many others, and that you in turn have helped form the thinking of the people around you.

Your mind reflects the consciousness of everyone from your parents and teachers to your heros and even authors who've opened your mind and added a point of view and comprehension that you've incorporated into your own. Those respective mind universes—*all* minds—keep connecting and reflecting on up to the universal mind of all minds and the universal flow of all information. This mother lode, of course, is what we're referring to as the psychic source. It's also what Jung called the collective unconscious. All information is interconnected and your mind contains the potential for knowing it all.

Think of how so many artists and designers seem to unconsciously plug into the same schools of thought at the same time. It's the same phenomenon that occurs when a particular movie or book—or even political leader—seems to resonate in everyone's minds, firing and reflecting everyone's own imagination.

When we resonate, we feel identification with information, a oneness with it. This is the natural state of uncommon sense, an all-encompassing state of timeless time and spaceless space. Perhaps the poet William Blake best described this state when he spoke of seeing "the universe in a grain of sand, and eternity in an hour."

Uncommon sense need not only be used to sense such weighty concepts as the universe and eternity, of course. *Any* object or detail in our lives contains the potential to connect us with a complete world of information. Exercise 19 will demonstrate just how easy it is for one small, everyday object to fully retrieve an entire experience and era for us.

EXERCISE 19: INTERCONNECTED FLASHBACK

Think of one meaningful object from your childhood—a teddy bear, a sled, a cup, a coat, anything—and note the flood of associations it unleashes.

See every detail and really feel what it is you remember. Do you feel the warmth of a childhood bed? Can you see the stripes on your mother's apron? Are you elated at seeing a gold star on your book report? Can you see yourself sadly clutching your sand pail on the last day of summer vacation? A whole world and a different era can be evoked by one seemingly insignificant object.

ONE FOR ALL AND ALL FOR ONE

We often experience a sense of wholeness with a larger life force. We sense ourselves as part of a larger group yet at the same time see the whole of that group reflected in ourselves—in the workplace, in our relationships, and in our recreational activities.

You'll know what I mean if you've ever played team sports or experienced a team spirit working on a project at school, on the job, in the military, or at camp. Here we see the whole-in-one in motion, as each person contributes his or her personal energy to the group until it begins to take on an energy of its own. Sometimes when a team of any kind really gets going, it's hard to remember who did what, and remarkably no one really cares because the whole is working as one.

Within our families we can see ourselves in the faces and actions of other family members. You may catch yourself repeating a phrase your mother used when you were a child. You may listen to your laugh and realize it sounds just like your father's. In the child, you can see the adult to be and the parent that was. In an adult, you can see the eternal essence of a child.

When we are with loved ones, we sense their moods and often empathize with them. It's important to take note of the special resonance you feel with loved ones. It's a sensation you'll expand upon to help you tune in to the people you work with or must deal with in everyday life.

EXERCISE 20: SEEING YOUR ECHO

Recall and record experiences of seeing yourself in others (family members, friends, lovers, colleagues) and seeing your particular situation reflected in those around you.

Is there a new turn of phrase you've picked up from your mate or that your mate has picked up from you? Does your child have a special way of cupping his or her chin in hand that stirs up memories of a long-forgotten habit from your own childhood? Does a friend from another background or part of the world nevertheless reflect many of your own personality traits?

Generate a good healthy list of these experiences in a notebook you designate your uncommon sense log. You'll probably be surprised to see how, after the first few notations, one "echo" echoes into the next almost naturally.

When you have plenty of material to work with, try to construct a composite self-description made up of qualities and traits you see in others. (Example: I have Dan's laugh, but one octave higher. I have the longer version of my mother's neat bob. I have my father's dry wit, combined with the silly limerick habit Jean and I developed together at summer camp. I have my grandmother's sturdy legs and strong sense of resolve, and my grandfather's high spirits. I have the new baby's dimples.)

To enrich your composite with additional qualities and details, go back to your original list and let it spark new whole-in-one echoes as needed. For extra inspiration, try drawing a featureless doll figure in your log and filling in each quality you discern as it comes up.

BEING A PART OF THE WHOLE PICTURE

Life is composed of many paradoxes. Perhaps one of the greatest is the fact that when we begin to access our uncommon sense, what we are doing, in effect, is simply finding out what it is we already know. Accessing uncommon sense is the process of making our own limited minds aware of the presence and resources of the unlimited universal mind.

You have already begun this process by balancing your energy with the energy of uncommon sense (as you did in Exercises 16 and 17). Now it's time for some firsthand exploration of the difference between your individual mind or self, and the larger part of you, or your own larger self that connects you to universal mind. Once you get to know your larger self you'll be that much closer to tapping into your natural pipeline to the "news" of the universe.

EXERCISE 21: SEEING YOUR LARGER SELF

Find a comfortable place where you will not be disturbed and where you have access to a mirror. Sit in front of the mirror or stand if you prefer.

As you look into the mirror, focus all your attention on your eyes. Stare into them as though they were someone else's. Study them carefully, looking for the inner face behind the physical mask. The eyes are truly the mirror of the soul, and you are looking for your inner essence, your larger self as opposed to your everyday self. Get up and walk around the room, maintaining your awareness of the larger you that exists behind your eyes.

Once you find your larger self on your own, repeat the exercise. Except this time, use a friend instead of a mirror to find the larger self in his or her eyes as he or she finds that self in yours. Discovering the larger self this way can often produce an eerie sensation—a sensation that really brings home to you how we are all quite larger than the bounds our everyday perception would suggest.

ON AND ON—THE NEVER-ENDING SAGA

All of our lives and all of life itself is interconnected, continually unfolding and enfolding us. Witness the ocean (long a symbol of universal consciousness) as its waves unfold, rush to the shore, return to the deep, and repeat the same process. Consider the changing of the seasons: fall into winter, winter reborn into spring, spring unfolding into summer, then fall, and over and over again. Notice the continual renewing of families as members are born, die, and live on in the stream of ancestors and descendants.

The development of our awareness follows the same pattern. Our awareness, too, is always evolving, and is always connected to the flow of universal awareness. Learn to experience your unique part in this flow, and you'll be rewarded with information that can help guide you through every aspect of your life.

LEARNING THE ABCs

FOLLOWING YOUR YELLOW BRICK ROAD

Now that you've begun to explore the flow, it's time to go directly to its point of origin—the source, which is waiting inside us and available at all times to supply us with unlimited awareness and information. Connecting with our uncommon sense is a natural matter of tuning in to our own inherent source-connection.

By looking within ourselves to find the source, we find, or rediscover, our own center. Feeling centered is really the sense of being connected to the source within. It's the sensation of being in perfect alignment with our own answers. In the end, the process of finding and connecting with the source comes down to discovering that we're already there. Finding the source means finding, or opening to, our own larger selves. To more readily and more clearly access this knowing or psychic self, we only need to *strengthen* our source-connection to it.

In this chapter, you'll be building up your source-strength by honing familiar skills you use every day. Get ready to greatly enhance your abilities to focus, to think and speak with intent, and to create clear mental imagery. By *whole focusing, affirming,* and *visualizing,* you'll naturally develop your uncommon sense and boost your ability to use it in everyday life.

It's important to keep in mind that the act of strengthening our source-connection and clear access to uncommon sense is a continual process. We're always connected to the source, of course, so at any moment we could experience its powerful information. However, becoming aware of this connection, and focusing on it more readily, takes time and patience.

As you practice the exercises in this book and your awareness itself evolves, you'll discover that your uncommon sense grows in its own way. Sometimes you'll find your answers are flowing. At other times, uncommon sense, and the source, seem nowhere to be found. But whether you're aware of it or not, each and every time you consciously connect, you're building up your ability to tune in to the source at will.

FOCUSING IN

Connecting to the source is impossible without focusing. If you've brought your undivided attention to any of the previous exercises, you've already used this technique. Focusing, quite simply, is the process of directing your awareness toward the source. The more finely you hone your focusing skills, the more clearly you allow uncommon sense to come into focus for you. Through breathing, relaxing, and concentrating, you'll learn how to focus like a pro.

THE BREATH OF LIFE

Breathing is more than a way to get oxygen into our lungs. Each breath is a reaffirmation of our connection to the source, and conscious breathing puts us in touch with the force of life itself.

You can actually shift the level of your awareness and your state of mind by changing the rhythm of your breathing. Ever notice how when you're afraid or angry you breathe in quick, shallow gasps? By taking ten deep breaths, as the old saying goes, it's quite possible to let go of those negative feelings. Doing so appeases the left brain's needs by giving it time to do what it does best—think. Then your deep breathing takes you beyond that, on to the intuitive right hemisphere, which has the chance of coming up with solutions that your left brain could never imagine. If ten simple breaths can help ease and open your mind so, just think of how much more you can accomplish, once you begin to spend a little more time putting your conscious attention to actively whole focusing.

The first focusing technique, "Breath Charge," is an effective, unobtrusive technique for tapping into your uncommon sense during the course of your day.

EXERCISE 22: BREATH CHARGE

Sit or stand in a comfortable position, making sure that your back is straight and well supported. Close your eyes and fully focus on your breathing process as you inhale and exhale three very deep—exaggeratedly deep—breaths. Really feel yourself release your breath on each exhalation. As you do so, you may start to sense a slightly lightheaded feeling. Once you're completely aware of your breath, continue to breathe deeply and rhythmically—not with the same level of exaggeration, but maintaining concentration on your breathing process.

Now place your right thumb on your right
nostril, effectively closing that passageway.
Breathe deeply and rhythmically in and out of
your left nostril. Now release your right
thumb, place your middle finger on your left
nostril and repeat the process.

Alternate nostrils at least three times, but
continue up to twelve repetitions if it feels comfortable for you to do so. By now you should
be feeling *really* lightheaded, so take it easy, go
at your own pace, and stop whenever you feel
it's right.

This exercise clears both sides of the brain.
It's a process that is used with great effect by
ancient yogis and modern business executives
alike. Try it at any time of day when you need
to clear your head. It will quickly release mental
blocks to open you almost immediately to the
flow of your uncommon sense.

RELAX!

Focused breathing leads to relaxation—something we all
could really use. It's especially important to feel relaxed
and to let go of whatever may be physically or mentally
inhibiting us from connecting to our own psychic resources. Bothersome mental monologues and persistent
kinks in the neck can be equally distracting. We've all
heard that the body is the temple of the soul. This trans-

lates into the need to keep your spine and neck relaxed because they form an all-important connecting passageway between the body and mind. And the energy of uncommon sense needs as clear a pathway, mentally and physically, as we can provide for it.

Most of us unconsciously seem to know that. Throughout the day we instinctively stretch and roll our necks so we can breathe easier and think more clearly. To consciously warm up for receiving uncommon sense information, we need to routinely practice neck rolls and spine straightening.

EXERCISE 23: NECK ROLLS

First start to breathe deeply and rhythmically just as you did in "Breath Charge" (Exercise 22). Now start to gently roll your neck. First roll it forward toward your chest. Then stretch it back a few times. Roll it a few times toward your left shoulder and then your right shoulder.

Go slowly. You may be holding more tension in this area than you realize—most of us have hidden knots of tension somewhere in the body, and this area is always one of the prime suspects.

There are two parts to the next exercise—one is more physical, and the second is more mental. Together they combine to relax and release the spine. Try both parts in tandem like a cat stretch first thing in the morning to help you start your day out right.

EXERCISE 24: SPINE STRAIGHTENING

SHOULDER PULL. Breathing deeply, bring your right arm up and then behind your head so that your right elbow is level to the crown of your head. Now touch the center of the top of your back with your right hand (it should be right there already).

With your left hand, gently pull your right elbow to the left until you start to feel a *very slight* pull in your right shoulder. Hold the stretch to the count of six, then relax, dropping both arms gently to your sides. Repeat on the left side.

Keep repeating until you "get" each shoulder at least three times. Feel the difference? I find this tremendously relaxing to do at any time of the day, especially when I'm feeling tight. It's great to know that opening to uncommon sense also feels so good!

SILVER STRING PULL. This is best done sitting in an upright chair, keeping the spine as straight as possible. Continue to breathe deeply, holding your head perfectly upright. As you breathe, begin to concentrate on the top of your head and breathe into the area, visualizing a silver string at the very center and top of your head that is gently and subtly pulling you upward and aligning both your physical body and your personal energy field.

Now sense your spine, head, and neck gently straightening, ever so subtly "raising" your head. Concentrate on "seeing" your spine straighten, as you continue your deep, relaxed breathing, allowing yourself to relax into this process instead of stiffening with it.

When you feel more aligned, return to your daily tasks, or proceed to the next exercise.

THE RELAXATION/CONCENTRATION CONNECTION, OR IN THE STILL OF THE MIGHT

Relaxation, of course, is also the process of release. When we relax, we release the fears, doubts, anxieties, and even physical sensations that stand in the way of our receiving uncommon sense messages. Relaxing is really a process of reconditioning the mind, as well as the body. When you relax, you open yourself to your own larger self by letting go of the mental baggage you carry in your everyday awareness.

We can find a good working example of this process in the world of the theater. How many times have you heard about performers who've experienced some kind of trauma right before taking to the stage, only to find themselves caught up in the "show must go on" tradition? Inspired to shift their focus away from their problems by the heat of the moment, such performers are able to go with the flow of their own performance, and not experience a break in that flow until the last curtain comes down. For each of us in all walks of life, some easy daily focusing can provide the same kind of wholehearted release and powerfully directed energy.

CONCENTRATION

After breathing, relaxing, and releasing, you really need to *concentrate* in order to complete your shift in focus from everyday awareness to the larger awareness of the flow. Concentration fine-tunes the process of tuning *out* everyday thinking to clearly tune in to the source's signal.

Tuning in means stilling our minds, and anyone who's tried to do this for any length of time knows that's not always easy. Suddenly thoughts come rushing in, vying for our attention like demanding, cranky children. The harder you try to focus and find peace, the more demanding and persistent they can become. These thoughts can range from mundane reminders like, "I've got to pick up the dry cleaning," to nagging doubts such as, "What the hell am I doing here?" You might recall a recent or long-forgotten memory; a lyric from an old song may pop into your mind, or you may hear a favorite melody or recall a scene from a movie or TV commercial.

You may even experience some anxiety as your left brain starts to feel left out. A fear of the unknown may grip you, as you leave the safety of logical left-brain thought, and move into a freer, floating awareness that feels new to you.

If you can relax into this feeling instead of fighting it you'll experience a pleasant, flowing sensation much like that of drifting off to sleep. Trust it and know you're not entering dangerous waters. Enjoy the trip, knowing you can flow along for as long as you like, and then return at will. Continue to breathe deeply and rhythmically. Allow yourself to experience the flow and the impressions you receive from it without thinking it over or analyzing it at all.

When thoughts *do* come up, don't fight your left brain. Resistance only gives energy to what you're resisting, creating a vicious circle of mental static. On the other hand, breathing into whatever you're thinking or feeling allows you to simultaneously let it go and open to a higher state of awareness. As you bring your awareness back to your breath, you'll find your thoughts floating to the back of your mind.

WHOLE FOCUSING

Now that we're relaxed and our minds are stilled, we're ready to take in powerful source information. Concentration enables us to open to this information whole-mindedly—letting awareness come to us without first mentally editing it. Remember, uncommon sense is *intuitive* sense—a flowing awareness channeled through your right brain in a whole new language your everyday awareness must relearn. So it's very important to let the information itself flow when you first tune in—simply, let it all come.

Later we can always bring in the left hemisphere to assess, analyze, interpret, and file what we've received. But the most important reason for developing our concentration is to allow the mind to open and receive without interruption or criticism.

You can easily experience whole-minded concentration with the help of a classic method used by practically everyone connecting with the source, from the most advanced yogis to beginning students in meditation and stress reduction. It's such a nonlinear exercise, it's a natural for opening to the flow of uncommon sense. You may find one or two experiences with it are quite enough to acquaint you with the experience of receiving information whole and that afterward uncommon sense flows to you in other ways. Or you may discover that this particular way of tuning in to nonlinear language is perfect for you, and you may want to keep doing it on a regular basis.

.   .   .

EXERCISE 25: WHOLE FOCUSING: AN EXERCISE IN CONCENTRATION AND CONTEMPLATION

Light a single white candle or select one beautiful fresh flower to focus on. Should you choose the candle, arrange to have a dimly lit environment so you can easily focus on its flame. In either case, the less visual or auditory distraction your environment contains, the better.

Bring your chosen object to your full attention, your full awareness. Really look at it. Drink it in with your eyes, letting any thoughts that arise float away as you concentrate on the candle or flower.

Keep focusing and breathing deeply and rhythmically. Your only goal is that of concentration. Try not to pay any attention to details. Simply breathe and take in the candle or flower as a whole. Continue whole focusing for at least two to five minutes.

After this exercise, you may feel very refreshed. Perhaps you may even have some kind of insight—a new idea, a hunch, or a new approach to a problem or situation. Or you may feel nothing. Never mind. Whatever the results, remember it's all part of the process, and your growing ability to concentrate without intellectual disruption is an important part of your overall developing inner fitness.

To increase your ability to access uncommon sense through concentration, try the whole focusing variation described in the next exercise. This exercise is an incredible energy booster. You'll probably feel relaxed afterward, and perhaps even recharged. I do this exercise myself before tuning in to a client because it opens up the channels almost immediately. I've also incorporated it into my daily routine, to continue keeping the channels open, and to continue to develop clarity. Try adding it to your routine, and see what just a few minutes a day can do for concentration, intuition, and creativity.

EXERCISE 26: WHOLE FOCUSING ON ENERGY POINTS

Instead of focusing on the candle or flower as you did in Exercise 25, choose one of three energy centers—your third eye, your heart, or your solar plexus—as your focal point. Breathe into the chosen point—again, the only goal being the focus itself. And, as before, do this for two to five minutes.

AFFIRMING THE CONNECTION

Our gentle but heightened focusing prepares the way for the second, more active form of concentration. This form of focusing fine-tunes and gives substance to our source-connection through words, creating a bridge between the seen and the unseen. The bridge is crossed through *affirming,* which is the act of expressing our intent to connect with the source.

An affirmation, either thought or spoken aloud, both confirms your perception of reality, and opens you to the larger reality of uncommon sense. Through affirmation you can make use of uncommon sense in your everyday life. If you've tried the energy-balancing exercises (16–18), you are probably already aware of the power of verbal affirmation.

FIRMING UP YOUR REALITY

We make affirmations every day, whether we're aware of them or not. Our very lives are affirmations of the way we perceive reality. Just as perceiving the source hastens our alignment with it, we will positively align or negatively align with whatever we perceive as truth in our daily lives. Say or think you aren't psychic or creative often enough, and *that* will be your reality. That's why it's so important to affirm, and keep affirming, the whole, unlimited truth of the source and your own reservoir of uncommon sense.

Luckily, we've all also been known to make spontaneous positive affirmations when we say things like, "Things have a way of working out." Far from being mindless filler, such seemingly casual affirmations can truly produce creative solutions to sticky problems. For instance, when a marketing expert I know is facing a difficult situation, he often finds himself repeating, "I know there's a way!" To the amazement of his colleagues, he generally pulls a solution out of the proverbial hat—helped by an opening line that has already affirmed his connection to the answer he seeks.

Try the following exercise to make you more conscious of the power of affirmation in your life. Start becoming aware that some of what you've been told, or even say or think yourself, may not be the whole truth, but just a misperceived part of that truth.

EXERCISE 27: WORD POWER

Lie or sit in a comfortable, distraction-free environment. Breathe deeply, slowly, and rhythmically, and start to think about your childhood. Recall a time when someone influential—a parent or teacher, or perhaps a friend—said something to you that eventually became an affirmation that you acted out. Perhaps it was, "How bright you are!" Or, "You know, you're not really very athletic." "You're not a joiner." "You're too sensitive." "I can always depend on you." "Your sister's the smart one—you're the pretty one."

Feel the pain of recognition? How close to your personal truth, past and present, are these affirmations? Do you still accept them as your personal truth? Know that you're now ready to accept, or not accept, any definition of your own reality at will.

Now look to your daily life, and observe how current affirmations are informing your sense of yourself. Become aware of statements, direct or indirect, made to you by your boss, loved ones, relatives, or others, as well as statements you find you are making yourself.

Do they reinforce the affirmations of your childhood? Do they represent a need for an improvement in your self-image? The more you can affirm positively in your everyday life, as well as in these exercises, the more powerful the positive reality of your enhanced intuition and creativity will be.

Your ability to create this reality is greatly upped by the positive structure you create for yourself, both in terms of your own affirmation routine and the affirmations of those around you. We all pick up the frequencies of others. That's why many people who are on the path of developing awareness choose to share experiences, and even exercises. In group settings, the positive energy is heightened, rewarding everyone involved with clearer information and increased awareness.

AFFIRMING RIGHT

Be aware at all times of the affirmations surrounding you and those emanating from you. You can probably do these exercises correctly for a few minutes every day, but if you spend the day's remainder in a doubtful, fearful, or otherwise negative state of mind, your earlier efforts will have practically gone to waste.

Think *acceptance*—of yourself and your own connection to the source. Think acceptance, too, of the process involved in making and strengthening it. Then think *repetition*—of your positively affirming that connection, and you've got the perfect recipe for "affirming right."

FORMING YOUR OWN AFFIRMATIONS

It's easy to apply the power of affirmation to your daily life. There are really only two simple guidelines. First, remember to keep every statement you make in the present tense, as in the eternal present of the source. Second, remember to make every statement positive, for it's positive reality you're seeking to align with. In other words, know and affirm that the intuition, creativity, and inspired guidance you seek is already there, and you'll surely find it.

. . .

EXERCISE 28: DO-IT-YOURSELF AFFIRMATION EXERCISE

As you keep in the present tense, and keep positive, you must also keep in mind that you're already connected to, and in the process of receiving, whatever you're affirming for. That's why most conscious affirmations start with the phrase, "I am."

"I am" is the open sesame of affirmation, which is why saying or thinking, "I'm so dumb," or "I'll never figure this out," can so powerfully influence the outcome of any situation. Instead, you'll want to follow "I am" with a statement of the most positive and unlimited possibilities. This, of course, is an affirmation of the unlimited power of the source.

Try, "I am now open to unlimited awareness/creativity/intuition/ . . . or fill in that blank with whatever it is you personally desire to affirm.

To reverse negative affirmations, such as thinking you don't have any answers, start off with the same positive "I am now" construction, and fill in the blank with something like, "I am now evolving in my awareness, and know that I am truly connected to all the information I need, whenever I may need it." Feel free to use the words that are most powerful and personal for you.

Always remember that the more fully you can accept, and affirm, your own source-connection, the more you can avail yourself of your own unlimited awareness. Once you have stated your desire or intent, know that its seed for manifestation has been planted; then—let it go! You've set into motion the powerful mechanics of the law of cause and effect. What you sow, you surely shall reap. You can keep your practice gentle but steady as you allow the source to process and nurture your verbalized intent. The more willing you are to trust this dynamic, the more quickly your answers will begin to flow from the source within toward your everyday awareness.

VISUALIZATION: GETTING THE WHOLE PICTURE

Focusing gently opens us to experiencing the source. Affirmation actively puts our intent into motion. *Visualization,* the technique that allows us to both receive and project clear mental images, is the final element we need to strengthen our uncommon sense reception. Within those images lies a wealth of information. Although different techniques appeal to different individuals, visualizing is perhaps the most powerful source-connector of all.

We all know firsthand from a lifetime of evenings spent in darkened movie houses the power that words and pictures possess when they are used in tandem. A movie may start from a screenplay, but the experience of words and images working so closely together is more than twice as vivid as dialogue alone. Visualization enhances the intent to connect that is expressed by affirmation, and also multiplies the power of that intent manyfold.

Visualization, like affirmation, is a powerful everyday reality shaper. Just as verbal affirmations determine your perception, conscious mental visualization will also shape and strengthen the way you view your life. The same bridge between the seen and unseen exists even when we use everyday expressions like "picture this" to describe a plan or a project that is eventually brought to life.

Sports psychology and medicine have known this for decades. In the 1920s a medical study proved that when patients concentrated on picturing a muscle move, it resulted in the actual experience of physical movement. Today, athletes use visualization to improve performance as a matter of course.

For instance, Olympic bronze medal figure skaters Jill Watson and Peter Oppegard have said they spend the final hour before a competition focusing their attention in from the outer reaches of the stadium to each other, their program, and, finally, the ice itself. Only once their vision is focused squarely on their best possible performance and away from the audience and judging panel, are they ready to do their best. High jumpers are trained to substitute the naturally daunting mental picture of the high hurdle with the much more constructive image of themselves sailing *over* the pole. The success of just such visualization methods has been verified again and again in articles about sports psychologists and in the winning performances of the athletes they advise.

Later we'll try some visual tuning exercises to add to your growing repertoire, but first let's examine the important role visualizing already plays in your everyday life.

MEMORIES AND IMAGINATION

The prospect of visualization can be intimidating to people who feel more kinship with a little voice inside them or with feelings than they do with visual images. Nevertheless, there are two basic sources of visual imagery that naturally flow through your life and that you avail yourself of each and every day.

Their names? *Memory* and *imagination*. Who among us has not conjured up the face of a far-off loved one, or the sight of last summer's gentle ocean shimmering with golden sunlight? Remembered visual images are often the most vivid substitute for the real thing, and the daydreams that overcome us in our everyday lives are often as richly visual as reality itself. It's quite easy to see the perfect dress or tuxedo for the party of your dreams, and certainly any children with imaginary playmates can tell you exactly what their friends look like, down to the last freckle.

Remembering and imagining give us spontaneous visualizing workouts that can clearly tune us in to our own uncommon sense. Every memory you experience confirms your innate power of visualization, and each flight of fancy you embark upon displays your potential for receiving powerful imagery from the source.

For our purposes the major difference between the ongoing flow of memory and imagination is that memories are images of events that have passed, whereas imagination pictures what has yet to come. In some cases, the imagining process creates pictures that are meant to live on only in the mind. In others, the process unveils events that do indeed come to pass. Within the context of the time/space continuum, the phenomenon of seeing realized experiences in advance is like going back to the future to access a memory of your forgotten past. Never mind if that seems confusing. In the search for uncommon sense, paradox abounds, and certainly no more so than in the process of visualization.

What are we to make of the imaginings that sometimes do and sometimes don't materialize? And how are we to tell the difference between the two types? Don't fear— you'll learn how in Chapter 5. For now, simply be aware of the important practical role your imagination may already be playing in your everyday life, and of the fluency in visual language you've already developed from a lifetime of remembering.

The next exercise will help you to explore just how easy it is to access a visual image, to sense all the rich information that initial picture contains, and to see for yourself how closely linked other kinds of impressions are to visualization.

EXERCISE 29: IMAGE POWER

Find a comfortable place that is free of distractions. Close your eyes, and begin to take deep and even breaths as you conjure up a favorite, powerful scene from nature—the ocean, the mountains, the desert at dawn.

See how easily and vividly that image comes to you, and once you have experienced it as a whole begin to explore the richness of its details. What colors do you see? Are there any shapes or visual textures you never noticed before? What particular elements of the natural setting give you pleasure, and what does the light tell you about the time of day? How does the air feel? What other sensory impressions do the details of your picture evoke?

Next, add your imagination. What would you like to be doing in this scene, or what are you doing in it? Get a sense of where things could go in the scene you have created. What do your thoughts tell you about yourself, about this image, or about what you would like to be doing?

Good. You have just used memory, daydreaming, and imagination to give you visually channeled information about yourself. Did you notice any difference between each sensation? More likely both the remembered and imagined parts of the scene had an equally rich reality. As you use visual images and other sensations to fine-tune your uncommon sense reception in Chapter 5, you'll find that accessing uncommon sense is quite similar to reminding yourself of a particularly vivid memory, and then exploring the insights that richly experienced visual picture has to offer you.

Please remember that visualization, like the total experience of developing uncommon sense, is itself a process that evolves gradually. Those feelings, little internal voices, and other sense impressions that may come to you more readily are, in fact, what I like to call "previsual visualizations." They are the stepping stones that will lead you to getting the big picture if you just go with the flow.

As more and more information starts coming into view it also helps to keep this in mind: Uncommon sense impressions of any kind do not tell us what to do or not to do. They *can* allow us to see, or otherwise sense, certain events or trends, and then, what is likely to happen if a particular trend is allowed to develop. We, ourselves, must decide what to do about whatever our uncommon sense shows us. Now, on with the show!

EXERCISE 30: DEVELOPING YOUR OWN PICTURE

Spend a few minutes doing the energy-balancing exercises as well as some deep breathing. When you feel relaxed and open, make sure your eyes are closed. Then visualize a blank white screen.

Continue breathing into the image as you picture that screen in all its detail. Maybe you're in a private screening room, or in front of your own TV. It is on this screen that your larger self will play the "movie of your future."

When the screen is bright and very clear, invoke your larger self by affirming, "I now open myself to my larger self. I allow whatever it wants to show me about my future to appear now."

Now you are ready to put yourself on the screen. First, flow with images of yourself until one particularly meaningful and familiar image comes to mind. If you do not receive a visual image right away, playfully flow with a particularly important feeling, phrase, scent, or any other impression until it transforms itself into a vision. Are you sitting in a children's playroom surrounded by toys? In an office, hunched over a desk? Do you see yourself as a cat, a swan, an oak tree?

When that first image is bright and clear, flow with it, as you did in the previous exercise, and see what new images and situations develop from that first source image. Do children come into the playroom to play with you? Do the piles of papers on the desk grow and grow until you're barricaded behind them? Is the swan gliding effortlessly toward an exciting new shore? Is the cat begging to be let outside for a good run?

Keep on flowing until the vision is complete. Don't edit or judge; just see what images come up. Later you can use the Visual/Feeling Checklist in Chapter 5 to interpret whatever symbols your images might present and pinpoint the message.

What did the images tell you about the way you perceive your reality? Can you take any action as a result of what you've seen? How would you like to revise the picture of your life so it reflects your desired reality? Just as you *received* images from your larger self about your life and its future, you can also *project* images you want to see about your own inner, and eventually outer, reality.

Run the movie again. This time you are the director. Add new images that shift the visual balance so it more accurately and positively illustrates your projected desire. Rerun the movie periodically. What has changed in the movie and in your day-to-day life? What has stayed the same? What visual elements would you like to add? Add them!

Now you've explored the three different means for clearly tuning in to—and strengthening—your source-connection. For most people, they work best in the sequence they've been presented here. But once you're familiar with the effects of each, you may find that a slightly different—or entirely different—sequence or selection works the best for you. Over time, you may also find you're better at particular techniques, and that some work better for you in certain situations, or when you're trying to access specific kinds of information. Follow your own guidance just as you follow the flow of uncommon sense, periodically checking in with your larger self to make sure you're making that connection just as clear and strong as it can possibly be.

PUTTING IT ALL TOGETHER

Now THAT YOU'VE LEARNED THE basic elements that make up uncommon sense you have all the practical tools you need to begin to receive and apply uncommon sense information. You're ready now to fine-tune your new skills and put them all together by learning how to "tune in," "get the picture," and interpret what you've got.

How exactly will you accomplish this? Well, first, you'll learn how to develop your natural sixth sense by developing the five you use every day. Next you'll try some easy techniques for learning to use those five senses in an altered—and enlightened—way. Your newly heightened senses will start picking up the pieces of your intuitive puzzle, and your uncommon sense will really go to work as you start to develop those little bits and pieces into whole, clear pictures—complete with accompanying story. Bit by bit, whole picture by whole picture, you'll come to know the whole truth of your own insights, creativity, intuition, and guidance.

Sound complicated? Relax! It's easier than you think. Remember to always warm up first (doing some neck rolls, deep breathing, and whole focusing for a bit), and then simply enjoy.

The first exercise, "Mind's Eye Imaging," builds on the visualizing ability you began to develop in Chapter 4. This is a really fun technique, and can be practiced alone or with a partner or even a small group. The technique of mind's eye imaging exercises your psychic visual muscle, strengthening your ability to receive uncommon sense and see the picture clearly in any situation.

EXERCISE 31: MIND'S EYE IMAGING

As always, start by getting comfortable in a tranquil, nondistracting environment, and warm up as suggested earlier. Next choose a magazine or an illustrated book (coffee table books work especially well) from your personal collection. After you've warmed up, thumb through the book or magazine with your eyes closed, and randomly let your hand rest on a page. Then affirm (either to yourself or aloud), "I now open my mind to the picture before me. I now allow the picture to develop in my mind."

In your mind's eye, see the white screen you first evoked in Exercise 30, "Developing Your Own Picture." Some people imagine themselves in an actual private screening room. Others see the white screen as a TV screen. Use whatever works for you. As you breathe into the image, gently allow any critical mental back talk to flow toward the periphery of your awareness and then disperse.

Next focus on the page your hand is touching, and let a picture develop on your inner screen. As always, allow whatever images that emerge to fully evolve without questioning, analyzing, editing, or judging. Explore these images, feelings, or other sensory details and note whatever comes up, paying special attention to your *first* impressions.

What similarities can you find between *your* picture and the one in the magazine? Is there a connection between colors, shapes, feelings, or moods? Did you see a fragment of one of the details of the image? Was your picture a simpler, perhaps symbolic version of the magazine picture? Did a feeling come along with your inner image and give you more information about the magazine picture? Remember, the point of this exercise is not to get it absolutely "right."

The *kinds* of correspondences you perceive will tell you a lot about your own personal uncommon sense language. You'll eventually learn how to fill out flashes using this language, and to translate those flashes into fully realized insights and solutions.

A look at others' experiences will help give you insights about your own. When one student of mine practiced mind's eye imaging, his inner screen revealed a picture of a lemon grove. The magazine illustration in question turned out to be a group of trees on a sunny day, and my student learned that for him lemons were a symbol for sunshine. In another class, we tried the first group variation described in Exercise 32. This time, the photo was one of a very peculiarly shaped vase of flowers, and one student instantly imaged a picture of a smoked ham hanging from a rafter. We all laughed when we realized that the ham was identical in *shape* to the flower vase. And my student made an important discovery about how his uncommon sense transmits messages to him.

You may perceive a color, a type of lighting, a feeling, or a sound that somehow represents the picture you're tuning into, or you may be one of the lucky ones who naturally receives accurate, complete pictures the first time out. Whatever your personal results, don't edit or criticize. Log in your impressions, especially your first impressions, and see what kinds of patterns come up.

If it's at all practical for you to do mind's eye imaging with a partner, or in a small group, make a point of trying the next two variations of the exercise. In a group situation you also have a chance to explore your ability to send, or project, visual images as well your ability to receive them. Secondly, the focused energy of groups greatly amplifies uncommon sense images and energy for all concerned. The experience can be positively exhilarating!

EXERCISE 32: MIND'S EYE IMAGING WITH A PARTNER OR SMALL GROUP

After you have completed your warm-ups, designate one member of the group as the sender. Have this person select a picture from a magazine or book. Then have everyone visualize a blank white screen in the middle of their foreheads. The sender will transmit the image to everyone else, just as a television signal is sent out to various TV sets from a broadcasting station. Meanwhile, the receiving partners will be seeing the image appear on their own screens. Before you begin, make sure everyone's screens are blank. Then have the sender focus on the chosen image first by staring at it and then visualizing it on his mind's eye screen. Have the sender concentrate on sending that image out to the rest of the group.

If you are the sender, try breathing into the middle of your forehead, consciously feeling and seeing the image going outward in a beam of light. If you are a receiver, watch what develops on your own white screen, just as you did in the first mind's eye exercise.

Note your impressions, especially your first impressions. Then switch roles until everyone gets a chance to send. Again, don't worry about what you "get," or about who sends or receives more clearly. Everyone has natural strengths, which can only be discovered through exploration.

EXERCISE 33: NATURE IMAGING

Choose who will send the image and who will be receiving it, just as you did in the previous exercise. This time, instead of looking in a book or magazine, have the sender transmit a familiar scene from nature to the rest of the group. The natural world can be seen as the original image of the source, and any time you send or receive its vistas you have the bonus of an extra strong and clear energy signal that boosts the vividness of the image.

After warming up, have the projector visualize a blank white screen while the other group members do the same. When all the screens are fully in place, ask the sender to project an entire scene from nature to the rest of the group. This scene could be a house on the ocean, a field of horses, a desert sunrise. Get as creative as you want. Concentrate on projecting the scene in all its detail. Is there an old pump behind the beach house? A bubbling brook running through the field? Are tiny rabbits hopping under the huge desert sky?

As in the previous exercise, the rest of the group will see what appears in their own minds' eye, note their impressions, and then take turns sending out scenes of their own.

It's not unusual in this exercise for each receiver to receive slightly different images—which contribute to the whole picture. For example, when I led one group in this exercise the image projected was that of a country house. At first, the images the receivers sensed on their own inner screens seemed to conflict. One student saw the shade of a thicket of trees develop on her inner screen. Another saw a low stone wall. A third experienced a very happy and serene feeling.

As it turned out, these seemingly different impressions didn't conflict at all. This particular house *was* shaded, and did have a stone wall in back, and it was the source of many fond memories for the sender. All three of these different impressions represented pieces of the original scene, and each complemented it quite accurately, without precisely duplicating it. Uncommon sense, it must be remembered, is a language of equivalents. As you learn to go with your *own* flow of visual, feeling, and other sense impressions, you'll eventually come up with your own complete equivalent of the big picture.

TALKING PICTURES

Earlier I said that pictures more than doubled the power of your verbal affirmations. Well, it works the other way around, too. Words make uncommon sense pictures more specific, and easier to interpret as a whole. In the process of narrowing and defining a scene, words also deepen and open it up, allowing us to see and understand it more fully.

Spontaneously talking out the pictures you receive really helps you to pinpoint their details. And every detail you narrow in on will open your picture up to receive yet another detail, and so on, creating a momentum that will really develop both your mental picture and your psychic self-confidence. As a form of affirmation, talking out also vastly improves your ability to *interpret* these developing pictures and make connections between uncommon sense imagery and the information it contains.

It's natural to feel somewhat bashful about spontaneously talking out your pictures. At some point, all of us
have been been told to think before we speak. Now is
certainly not the time to give in to those feelings, however. Especially as you're beginning to learn how to develop uncommon sense, it's very important not to think
first, but just go with the flow of describing what you see
as you see it, even if the images aren't quite clear yet. This
will help them develop more clearly. I promise! Here's
how it works.

EXERCISE 34: TALKING PICTURES

Warm up in a comfortable place, and try mind's
eye imaging, with a partner or on your own.
When you reach a plateau in your image reception, spontaneously describe what you are seeing, without wondering whether what you're
saying is right or wrong.

If you're working with a partner, ask your
partner for confirmation (in the case of the ham
and the vase, your partner would have said,
"Yes, that's the same shape as the image I'm
projecting"). If you are working alone, simply
ask your larger self the same questions. It will
give you the answers that you need, and your
own mental verbalization will spark the same
focusing and opening process.

Let's go back to the case of the vase and the

ham again to watch this technique in action. Put yourself in the place of my student. Now that you've described your initial picture of a ham and know that it represents a shape, your inner screen will open to receive more information. At this point, you might see a shiny white surface, or bits of yellow light above the shape. Or you might feel that the shape has a cool smooth surface. You may even put all of these fragments together and develop the picture of a table lamp.

Again, ask for confirmation by telling what you see as you see it, without judging or editing. In this case, your partner might tell you the object is not a table lamp, but that it does sit on a table, and it does have a ceramic base. This specific, focused information might inspire you to revise the image in your mind. Perhaps you'd even pick up a delicious fresh fragrance, and suddenly discover the true identity of the picture.

Always continue this process of spontaneous give and take until any inner image is complete. Record your experience to find more patterns and connections later. With practice, you'll find you can even receive and interpret images and feelings quite fluidly, translating from one idiom to another almost simultaneously in your mind. This is what professional psychics do.

Even though it takes time and practice to develop this level of proficiency, you may even now experience the occasional flash when symbol and interpretation seem to come to you together.

Once you get good (and it won't take long), try the following variation on talking pictures as you go about your day. It's especially useful whenever you're trying to get more information than meets the eye, say at an auction, or when you're trying to size up a potential date.

EXERCISE 35: X-RAY VISION, OR SEEING BETWEEN THE LINES

First, create a blank white screen in your mind's eye and mentally ask your larger self to fill the screen with images of the reality of a given situation. You can do this with your eyes open.

Once the fragments and symbols are present, mentally ask your larger self, "What else is in the picture?" or, "Show me more." It shouldn't take long to complete an X-ray picture of the situation.

What sort of information did you access? Keep developing the picture until you're satisfied, talking it out with your larger self as you go along. The more precisely you've learned to pinpoint specific images in mind's eye imaging, the more precisely you'll be able to find the practical answers you need.

Here's a fun phone exercise to practice that develops your imaging prowess while providing practical information.

EXERCISE 36: PICTURE PHONE

As your caller speaks, take a few deep breaths, focus on your mind's eye, and see the inner blank white screen that will allow you to turn your phone into a "picture phone." You may also think to yourself, "I'm now tuning in to the picture and opening to the images on the screen."

See what images develop. For example, try to see what the person is wearing, and look for colors and moods. You may get images or feelings of "hot" or "cold," "up" or "down," for example. These could relate either to the colors being worn or what your subject is feeling at that moment. A color that you see in a flash could also contain a symbolic message. Check the energy color references in Chapter 3 for possible interpretation.

Listen to your caller's voice: What does it tell you? What images does it evoke? Can you sense your caller's physical environment? If it's one you're already well acquainted with, try to tune in to what may be different about it that day. Perhaps it contains a new piece of furniture. Maybe the room is especially clean or untidy, or is in some other way changed. Try to casually obtain confirmation by asking how your caller is feeling, or simply by asking what's new, *after* you've gotten the picture.

THE VISUAL/FEELING CHECKLIST

By using talking pictures and mind's eye imaging, you've probably gotten to know something about your personal psychic style. You may have had visual flashes that give you a feeling, or you may hear sounds that tell you something important about what you feel. Uncommon sense pictures tend to fill in as one sense impression or detail flows into another until the full message is complete.

Checking in on all the different messages a single picture may contain by checking in with all your senses will go a long way toward interpreting those raw bits and pieces of uncommon sense. The Visual/Feeling Checklist is an easy, effective tool to use along with talking pictures to develop and interpret your uncommon sense pictures. Many people find that talking pictures is best to help flesh out those important first impressions, and the checklist is terrific for interpreting and enhancing pictures already in progress. Try it out, get to know it, and feel free to refine it according to your own needs.

As you receive images via any of the techniques in this chapter, ask yourself the following questions, each time checking in with your larger self for more details.

VISUAL/FEELING CHECKLIST

1. Are there *people* in this picture? How many people are there? Who are they? What are they doing? Are you there? Is someone or something entering the scene or leaving it? Is this person moving quickly or slowly? What does this emphasis mean to you? Example: If you are in the process of hiring a new employee, you may tune in and see one candidate moving quickly out in front of the pack. This information could help you discover the winning candidate, and also indicate that the one you choose will really take the lead on the job.

2. What are the *feelings* of the people in the scene? If you are in the scene, how do you feel? How do others feel? Is the general feeling of the scene lively, friendly, slow, quiet, tense, staid, youthful? Does it feel—literally or figuratively—hot, cold, wet, dry?

Example: Perhaps you see yourself in the middle of London on a foggy day. Even amidst the cold and wet, though, you feel truly buoyant. This might be your sign that there is joy just on the other side of the big gray cloud you've been living under.

3. Are you seeing an *image* in the foreground of the picture or in the background? Is this a wide angle image or is it a closeup? What does the focus of the picture emphasize and deemphasize?

Example: If there are adults in the background, and a roomful of kids' toys and clothes in the foreground, that could mean you will soon be spending a good deal of your time with children.

4. What are the *colors* in the picture? Are they bright? Muted? Pale? What do these colors symbolize?

Example: A vibrant blue airplane could mean someone's about to take off creatively. For more color symbolism, see Chapter 3.

5. What's the *environment* of your picture? Is it an outdoors scene? Indoors? Is it set in the city? The country? The city you live in? A foreign country? What can you see or sense at the periphery of the image? Mountains? A grove of olive trees? Ocean? Could the scene itself be a symbol?

Example: As you tune in, you start to see the ocean very clearly. The ocean often symbolizes the unconscious, and so could either indicate your own process of exploring your personal inner depths or a journey you're about to take to the literal seashore.

Note: Here, as with other impressions, keep records of the kinds of things that come up in order to find personal patterns and what significance they hold for you.

6. What do you *hear* in the scene? Are people talking? What are they saying? Are the voices angry or gentle? Is there any other sound—a whistling wind, a waterfall, bird song, the sound of traffic, a buzz, or a hum? If there is music, what kind of music is it? A traditional war song? A love song? A nursery rhyme?

Example: You suddenly hear the song phrase, "I'll be seeing you in all the old familiar places..." It could mean the scene is taking place in the 1940s, or it could be giving you information about a lost loved one who is coming back into your life. Use the other questions on the checklist to tell you which meaning might apply.

7. What are your *feelings* as you tune in—how are you responding? Are you anxious, joyful, at peace? Are you feeling surprised, helpful, disappointed about the outcome of the situation?

Example: When I was tuning in to one client, I had such a feeling of happiness I almost jumped for joy, and knew the situation we were examining would turn out positively. With another client who'd just been unfairly fired, I felt his shock, and then a slight pain in my heart as I realized he was going to have some heartbreaking near-misses with other work opportunities. But then I felt a sort of calm after the storm, followed by a feeling that clinched a sense of resolution, as I experienced a happy internal explosion, like Fourth of July fireworks. Happily, I could tell him that things would not only calm down—crises usually do—but, in fact, his career would eventually be flying sky high.

Note: It's important when you get any feeling, but especially a negative one, to see or feel what comes next so you can not only fill out the picture, but come to a better sense of resolution.

8. Are you experiencing any *other physical sensations:* textures, tastes, smells? There may be a very strong floral scent, or the smell of the ocean, or garbage.

Example: Smelling a fire could clue you in to an incendiary situation. Sensing a bitter taste might deliver an uncommon sense pun, indicating that an event will leave a bad taste in your mouth.

9. What *time* is it? Is there something about the lighting in your picture that can tell you the time of day? Is there a clock in the scene? If you get a number, you'll have a great opportunity to pin your larger self down. Ask what the number means. Three months? Three days? Three years in the past, the present, or the future? Are there furnishings, clothing, a season of the year, or forms of transportation (horse and buggy, automobile) that give you a clue?

Note: Since time is a continuum, it's one of the hardest types of information to pinpoint and develop. You may find as you log things that certain feelings simply mean "sooner" or "later" to you. The best way to narrow down that elusive time frame is to keep asking your larger self specific questions: Ask how many days, months, or years you've moved into the past or future. Continue to ask until you're satisfied.

If you get a picture unaccompanied by a time sense, it may take that first impression a very long time indeed to materialize. When I first met my husband I "tuned in" and saw him working on a children's project. For *six years* I continually saw that project. Finally, now what I'd seen—and kept seeing—has finally started to come his way, as he's finding himself working on both children's television shows and advertising for kids.

After you get familiar with the checklist, you'll notice you get very clear frequent information in some areas and less in others. That's good! Using the Visual/Feeling Checklist doesn't only help you to fill in your pictures. It also helps you pinpoint your own personal psychic style. For instance, one of my clients always perceives information as events going on in rooms. Another always perceives information as a movie. Still another habitually hears people talking, and develops images to fill out the scene of these overheard conversations.

Eventually, you may want to drop some of the questions from your routine as you discover the kinds of perceptions that guide you most clearly and strongly to more detailed information. You're probably also likely to find that by tuning in to *one* particular sense or sensation—smelling a particular scent, hearing a certain song, feeling a sense of heat, for example—and allowing it to flow, it will naturally lead you to a picture rich with all kinds of sensory details.

Pay especially close attention to the feelings that accompany any picture: They work hand in hand and can hold the key to the impressions you receive. For instance, a student of mine was talking to his brother when he had the very strong sensation his brother was going to be involved with a nightclub.

He asked him if this was a possibility, and his brother said that he had been approached to consult in such a business. As my student tuned in further, he began to see a rosy color and started to feel warm and happy, which showed him that this project was likely to happen, and that it would be very positive.

Take special note of resurfacing pictures—they're the most likely to occur in your real life. Just as conscious picturing of the same scene or idea will strengthen its reality, images repeatedly making appearances without any effort on your part have a very, very strong chance of being realized. Conversely, at some point, you may try to receive information about a future project or situation, and you won't be able to see yourself doing it at all. There could be a message there for you, too.

Now that you've got your intuitive perceptions all checked, how do you make sense of them? Here's a perfect example of how the Visual/Feeling Checklist helped one particular client. She used it to combine the bits of data she received through her different senses into a single clear and ultimately very useful picture.

My client had been trying to determine what was going on with a corporate client of her own. She started tuning in with her uncommon sense when she felt uncertain about her continuing business relationship with the company. The first image she received was that of a huge, bright graphic design, which seemed so loud and wild it almost blinded her mind's eye. She had a feeling it represented the general tone of the company, but she wasn't quite sure if it suggested dynamism or confusion.

As she went through the Visual/Feeling Checklist, the phrase "Glory Hallelujah" sprang into the picture. These words didn't seem to go with the picture at all, so she focused on them until they developed into the lyrics of the famous Civil War song "The Battle Hymn of the Republic."

My client went through an entire verse in her mind, in an attempt to find any possible significance. The South had nothing to do with her picture, nor did religion or the Civil War period in history. Suddenly, as she finished the verse, she came to the realization that the song was really pointing to a *corporate* civil war—the power struggle that was going on within the company itself. The original picture she'd received now made perfect sense. The company she was working with was indeed both energetic and confused. Each piece of the picture really confirmed and helped interpret the information provided by the other.

Note: If you find yourself receiving a multiplicity of images and sensations, and it all seems too confusing, tune in to those which seem stronger and brighter. Those will be your most likely message-providing candidates.

GETTING THE STORY

From time immemorial, we have been intrigued by the details of other people's lives. The ancient, ongoing art of storytelling demonstrates our primal need. With the help of finely tuned pictures, words, and all kinds of uncommon sense feelings, you can tune in to the true stories of anyone you choose (including your own, of course). Storytelling, uncommon sense style, will help you fine-tune this skill and develop your overall inner knowledge.

You've probably already practiced storytelling whenever you've read a particularly evocative passage in a book. Who can read their favorite authors without mentally filling in the details of a particularly vivid and beloved scene? Furthering the story yourself and taking off from a narrative master's setting is not only fun—it's easy.

If you've ever whiled away time on a movie or grocery line creating lives for the interesting strangers you see around you, and thought, "Gee, I wonder what his story is," then taking that process one step further and creating your *own* setting for psychic storytelling will be easy, too.

EXERCISE 37: STORYTELLING

Focus on someone who is waiting on line, or on someone sitting at another table in a restaurant—or choose any stranger or acquaintance who inspires you. Create your white screen. Obviously, if you're in a public place you can't do the full warm-up. Just breathe deeply a few times and continue breathing into the screen you've visualized in your forehead.

Next, talk to your larger self about your subject. A casual question along the lines of "I wonder what her story is?" will affirm your connection with the answer and send information through. Or, think to yourself, "I am now tuning in to the highest information and getting the full story." Use the Visual/Feeling Checklist and talking pictures as the information starts to flow.

Once it does, try asking your larger self pinpointing questions. For example, "Is this a passionate person, or a cool cucumber type? Is she or he happy or sad? Is she or he cynical or optimistic? Liberal or conservative? In a relationship or single? A native or an out-of-towner? A pet owner? A parent? The list of questions is infinite. Let yourself flow with whatever seems to be in the proper line of questioning at the time, and continue to flow with the pictures, feelings, or other insights you begin to conjure up.

It's natural to wonder how much of your "story" goes beyond the obvious. It's easy to get certain impressions about a person whose coat is covered with cat hairs, or about someone who looks sad and bedraggled. Plain old common sense you say? Well, the point of developing your uncommon sense is to integrate it with your everyday skills of elementary deduction. When you answer everyday questions you always have the option of going for the most obvious solutions. What uncommon sense does is train you to see more clearly both in terms of what's staring you in the face, and in terms of the unseen answers below the surface, to give you the complete picture of any situation.

The ultimate in uncommon sense integration is realizing that whatever answer you're seeking is already inherent in the question. This bypasses having to tune in to a question or problem altogether, and allows you to go straight to the answer or solution. Professional psychic counselors use this technique all the time.

EXERCISE 38: FINDING THE ANSWERS IN THE QUESTIONS, PART I

First, warm up. Then have a friend or friends write a question on a slip of paper. Make sure each person writes down his or her *own* question. Phrase questions to avoid yes or no answers. For instance, instead of asking, "Will I go to Bermuda this winter?" ask, "What will happen with my winter vacation?" Tell friends to concentrate on the question and its desired answer while they write their questions out. This will sharpen your own focus and help you to tune in to the information they need.

If you're working with a group, have your friends fold their completed questions in half so that the handwriting is hidden, and place them in a container from which they can be blindly selected one at a time. If you're working with one partner, don't worry about anonymity. I've even used this technique to answer questions for myself.

By now, we're all familiar with the stereotypic image of a turbaned swami holding a written question to his forehead. Well don't laugh, but you may be employing that technique yourself next! Select one of the handwritten questions and hold it to your third eye energy center—or, if you prefer, to your heart or solar plexus. Experiment with all three, because most people find they are more receptive in one of the three locations. Also, you may find that for different kinds of questions you bring the paper automatically to a different energy center.

Don't even try to tune in to the hidden question that is written on the paper. Tune in to the *answer* instead. Say to your larger self, "I now allow the answer to unfold." Watch the picture develop on your white screen if you're using the third eye point, feel it developing through your emotions if you're holding the question to your heart, and experience the answer as a gut sense of knowing if you have chosen the solar plexus.

As impressions start to come up, freely ask for confirmation from your larger self and, of course, from the person you're tuning in to. As always, try talking it out immediately, taking off from your first impressions and allowing them to flow into a more complete answer.

Then use the Visual/Feeling Checklist to pin-point information. (*Note:* Don't worry if the senses you experience are different at various points than those listed here. This is only a general guideline.)

EXERCISE 39: FINDING THE ANSWERS IN THE QUESTIONS, PART II

You can use the same technique as Exercise 38 with questions posed over the telephone. This is a little more advanced, but there are people who respond psychically more strongly to the sound of a voice. It's certainly easy enough to try in the course of your day to find out. Again, tune in with and to your white screen, see what comes up, and don't let it bother you if this method produces fewer results. You can also try having someone ask you a question face to face. These last two variations are probably quite similar to what you do when you sit around talking with friends or family anyway. They simply provide a deeper, more informed way of providing people you care about with guided answers, and a technique you can really apply very unobtrusively and practically in daily life.

The next exercise offers a way of reading

objects and will introduce you to the technique
I use as a professional psychic. The ancient and
timeless craft of psychometry uses a very basic
technique to achieve powerful results in our
contemporary world. Psychometry will provide you with highly guided information about
others and should be practiced with a partner or
in a group.

EXERCISE 40: PSYCHOMETRY

Do your warm-ups. Then ask your partner or
the first group member to give you a metal
object that touches his or her body constantly:
a ring, watch, other item of jewelry, or even a
well-used key. A metal watch with a leather
band is fine; so is a piece of jewelry that also
contains precious stones. It's also best, though
not absolutely crucial, to use an object no one
but your subject has worn or used.

Hold the metal object in your hand as you
instruct your partner to ask you a question that
does not have a yes or no answer, just as you did
in the last exercise. Next, tune in to your mental
screen or feelings and concentrate on the answer as you pick up on the personal energy that
has naturally been transferred to the object in
your hands. The metal acts as a powerful con-

ductor, as Ben Franklin demonstrated with his famous kite and key.

Talk out the answers you receive with your partner or the group without judging or editing, paying special attention to first impressions. Ask for confirmation, then keep on going until the answer feels complete.

EVERYDAY PSYCHIC OPTIONS

It's easy to check in with your uncommon sense as you go about your day. Whether you need a quickie answer to an urgent question or simply want to integrate uncommon sense with your normal work routine, you can do so freely and unobstrusively whenever you feel the urge.

EXERCISE 41: THE ONE-MINUTE PSYCHIC

This technique is specifically designed for sizing up any situation in a flash. Use it whenever you need it—during your work, socializing, traveling, or any other situation where time is of the essence.

Warm up by taking a few deep breaths, and focus on your white screen. Quickly ask a question of your larger self, and check your very first impression of the answer with the Visual/ Feeling Checklist. For instance, before you open the door to an important meeting you might want to ask, "Which tone should I take for my presentation?" This technique will help you to make an uncommonly educated choice in any situation.

Your uncommon sense will always offer invaluable, instant insight on how to gently realign an approach or make a decision that will be just right and just what you need at the time.

There are moments in your life when you have much more time to tune in to an enlightened answer. Do all the warm-ups you need before you visualize your white screen, or whole focus on your feelings to see what impressions you receive. In addition to any of the previous exercises, you might want to use a technique that I personally enjoy. Try writing a letter to your larger self as though you were addressing an advice column. You'll get an illuminated answer to any of your questions—from the most mundane to your most soul searching.

The more regularly you can maintain a balanced program of inner workouts—especially if it includes deep breathing, energy balancing, whole focusing and, of course, a record of your impressions, the more fine tuned and immediately available your uncommon sense will be.

PROCESSING: PUTTING IT ALL TOGETHER

Tuning in to, and getting your answers on a regular basis, you must remember, is a process. Even when you don't think you're getting anywhere, in fact you really are. For instance, when I first began to develop my psychic ability I had a vision of myself as a ballerina spinning merrily. One of my teachers had a telling interpretation of that image: He told me it meant that at the time I was "moving," or growing, very quickly, and I should really enjoy the spin, because eventually a time would come when I would appear to be not moving at all. The time did come, and I indeed felt like I was stuck in molasses.

When your own development seems so slow you feel as if you're making no progress, it's important to remember that the process of developing your uncommon sense takes place on many different levels of awareness. So no matter where you think you are, on a deeper level you're still learning and absorbing.

As you open, and continue to open, to the total awareness of the source, you'll extend your own growing awareness beyond mere data gathering. Slowly but surely, you'll also be evolving empathy—the ability to identify with and find the feelings contained in the facts. Added to your quick-tuning skills, the ability to empathize will allow you to more deeply understand and fully complete the big picture. Developing empathy does take longer and is a more subtle process. When you're feeling frustrated, know your empathy is probably strengthening and deepening at that very moment.

Whenever you're tuning in to your own or other people's questions, be sure to look for emotional meaning in any answer you intuit, so that you can apply that answer in a caring way. Think of the difference between a sympathetic doctor and a cold just-the-facts technician. Always ask your larger self, as you're receiving impressions, "How can I use this information to *help*?" Guidance and accurate information received together make for a total picture—wholly and clearly received, and wholly useful in life.

No one has more uncommon sense than anybody else, but we each have an individual path to uncommon sense that unfolds in its own way. Everyone will find that certain methods will reap more accurate answers and certain types of information will come through much more clearly than others. You might be better at tuning into medical information, or you may discover your gifts apply best to counseling, or finding lost objects or people. Similarly, you might turn out to be a better sender of uncommon sense information than a receiver.

You may also find you have very quirky talents. For instance, when I was a child, one of the very first signs I had of my psychic sensitivity was when I began to sense what second language someone spoke. As you read this book, you may also realize that you, too, have a special little talent that could show you an area in which you have a particular uncommon sense strength, or may show you the way to many more fertile areas to come.

HOW DO YOU KNOW WHEN YOU GET A REAL ANSWER?

Remember that getting and knowing your answer is all part of an ongoing process. You'll get lots and lots of impressions before one develops to the point of certainty. Those first impressions, of course, are the ones that could be the most true and meaningful. Let them all flow, though, without analyzing or editing, and note the strongest, clearest, and most complete.

Do you feel a slight shock of recognition when that right impression comes along? Feel a tingle? Or even chills? Do you feel, or hear, the ring of truth? Or do you experience a feeling of perfect harmony or balance when it suddenly feels right? Does your heart beat a little faster? Your breath seem taken away? Do you feel it as a gut instinct, or does it in some other way hit you where you live emotionally?

Of course, the ultimate form of confirming your information is to actually see it come true. When an event you foresaw manifests in real life, it's not only proof positive of your uncommon sense, it's proof that what you'd tuned in to was an absolutely correct answer.

You may find certain types of answers you get manifest more than others, or you may get a partial answer that only makes sense when the full answer finally material-izes. A client of mine is currently having a feeling that's very general. She senses that somehow, in some way, she'll be involved with counseling at colleges. No impression other than that first one is very specific right now, but she knows that when the time is right she'll start seeing exactly how it all is going to occur.

It's also quite common to experience what I call the "right church/wrong pew" phenomenon. Another psychic I know once got a flash of a friend looking at slides, and kept seeing the word *agency* somehow connected to that image. He thought for sure she would wind up behind an advertising agency desk. Later, she did do a little free-lance work in that area, but the slides turned out to be the pictures from her honeymoon—with her new husband, an advertising executive!

You, too, can and will find your confirmation waiting for you—messages are everywhere you look. With practice, anytime and anywhere you'll be open to their guidance. The exercises in this book aren't meant to just give you proficiency at certain times in certain situations. They'll permit you to apply what you've experienced to all avenues of life.

Pay attention to things like subway signs, overheard conversations, movie or TV dialogue, songs, or that fragment of something someone says to you that suddenly sets off an aha! inside your head. Remember the magic of synchronicity? Perhaps you've been thinking about going to France, and suddenly everywhere you go, people keep mentioning France. This could be a form of needed confirmation. Everyone seems to have an area where confirmation suddenly comes in. Some see weather changes as a sign, or get a sense of acknowledgment from a song that contains a significant phrase being played "by chance" in a restaurant or on the radio.

WHAT DO YOU DO WITH AN UNCOMMON ANSWER?

An uncommon answer comes with an inherent directive—apply and integrate it! That means if you get a message during your daily whole-focusing session, or at any other time, put the answer into motion, but if and only if that makes sense for you. Remember, we're going to be using our *common* sense, too. If your answer isn't meant to be used at that moment, put it on your mental back burner to see what more develops as you continue to clarify the message with your larger self. Maybe it isn't meant to be put into motion at all. Only you will know, now or over time.

If you receive information about someone else, use your common sense to decide whether or not you should give it out. Your developing awareness needs to be supported by a sense of responsibility. With your own evolving sense of infinite wisdom, you must ask yourself responsibly if the person will benefit from this information. How can you communicate it in a considerate way?

THE SPIRAL OF AWARENESS

As you continue the process of developing uncommon sense, remember it's not a linear progression moving from one definite point of awareness to another. Instead, all the many different stages of your development, and the many different levels of awareness you experience, are incorporated into *one* ever-increasing awareness.

Developing awareness has a spiral, upward movement that allows you to see both where you've been and where you are at the same moment, and to perceive the inherent connection between the two. Sometimes, the integration process can be a slightly bewildering one. There may be moments when you actually sense the light at the end of the tunnel and at the same time still feel in the dark.

Just remember in those situations there is indeed an answer, but for whatever reason you're not quite ready to see it yet. You will keep on adding to your overall enlightenment as you spiral up in awareness. Soon you'll be able to re-experience a dark moment with a new ray of understanding. This is very much like the experience we've all had as children when our mothers told us, "You'll understand when you're older." Of course, when we matured, we were able to comprehend more from the vantage point of our broadened knowledge and experience.

Rest assured that if you're still a bit hazy about developing uncommon sense, your understanding is guaranteed to clear and widen. You'll gain confirmations and answers to your deepest questions as you yourself continue to develop, to grow, and to—in the truest sense—know.

UNCOMMON CREATIVITY

THE CREATIVE FORCE IS WITH YOU

When you access your uncommon sense, you also open up all sorts of creative floodgates. Intuition and creativity are very much related—they're both natural resources of the right brain. In many ways, if you develop one quality, you naturally develop the other. That's why highly creative people are also highly intuitive, and vice versa. You can add flowing creativity to the abounding benefits you gain from developing your uncommon sense. In fact, if you've begun to practice any of the exercises in this book, you've already started to tap your own reservoir of creative expression.

Since we are all connected to the ultimate creative expression, the source, we all have an innate ability to express ourselves creatively. Just as our source-connection makes us all naturally intuitive, it also allows us all to be natural artists.

We may not all be working painters or musicians. But we do each express ourselves creatively in our professional and personal lives when we juggle schedules, put together deals, write speeches or papers, decorate rooms, and otherwise problem solve. Each time we use our wits to complete a less than mechanical task, we're allowing ourselves to be guided by an intrinsic linkup to the creative force.

Creative thinking is whole thinking, and being creative is our way of getting in touch with the whole of creation. We feel balanced or in tune with our whole selves when we engage in any creative activity. Just as the answer is inherent in the questions you ask yourself, the creative solution is already present in the whole of the creative project.

Consider the great Michelangelo's approach to the sculpting process. He felt his task was "merely" to uncover the perfect finished figure that already lay within a block of stone. In the same manner, an artist is already inside of you. You can contact this artist anytime. In fact, unknowingly you already do. The more you consciously open to the creative force, the more your own creative genius will unfold, inspire, and inform you. Try the following exercise whenever you sit down to do creative work or problem solving.

EXERCISE 42: TAPPING THE ARTIST WITHIN

Breathe deeply and visualize yourself surrounded in glowing white, blue, or aqua light.

Next, breathe into the energy point in your throat, heart, or mid-forehead, whichever of the three feels best to you.

Affirm mentally or out loud, "I now allow the creative force to flow and express itself through me. I am the channel for its perfect expression."

Remain still and relaxed and continue breathing into the energy point of your choice for a few more moments. Then start to work, allowing your ideas to flow, without judging and editing, as bits and pieces, or whole information, start to come. Keep working as long as you feel inspiration flowing, bearing in mind that you can judge or evaluate what you've got after you've followed that flow.

CREATIVE THINKING IS ALTERNATE THINKING

Now that you've learned how to tap into your natural reservoir of creative energy, it's time to really work out your creative muscle. Both professional psychics and artists look at the familiar world in a new, or alternate, way, with illuminating results. That's exactly what you are learning to do, too, every time you take the leap of faith to open to uncommon sense. Practicing taking the leap of alternate thinking will also allow more of your creative potential to leap forth.

Artists are taught that any picture consists of more than just the subject painted or photographed. It is the dynamic of the negative space—the space around those subjects, and combined with them—that makes up the whole picture. The following exercise will help you develop more complete awareness of the negative space surrounding and informing everything, increasing your ability to think alternately, and create wholly.

EXERCISE 43: SEEING THE NEGATIVE SPACE

First, choose a highly graphic black or white print or photograph from a newspaper, magazine, book, or postcard collection. Now look at the picture as you normally would, concentrating on the generally darker and foregrounded subjects. For example, focus on trees against a sky, people in a room, and so on.

Next reverse the process. Concentrate on everything in the picture except for what you just looked at, as if these parts of the picture were jigsaw puzzle pieces that connected with the parts of the scene that normally catch your attention. Then close your eyes and look again at the whole picture, giving both the positive and negative parts equal importance. Notice how they all interrelate.

Try the same exercise to enhance your perception of the true nature of your everyday life; look at food on a plate, furniture in a room, objects on a desk, and so on. I guarantee your point of view will be greatly enhanced and you'll start feeling more creatively and intuitively informed next time you sit down to read between the lines of one of your own projects.

Humor is another great alternate-thinking creative tool. The best comedians have an offbeat view of the world, which interprets the stuff of everyday life in a wacky, refreshing way. As a comedy writer has said, "Humor is seeing all three sides of the coin."

Laughter itself is like the wholehearted release of focused breathing. It actually changes our level of awareness, lightening it and releasing whatever else is on our minds. So don't forget to laugh at yourself every now and then. Let yourself get into that playful, fertile, alternate state of mind.

Here are some more exercises and games to help you think in alternate ways, and connect with your own natural talent for creative thinking.

EXERCISE 44: WORDSPIN

Take a word. (For the sake of an example, we'll use the word *hot.*) Spin off verbally from that original word without using synonyms or antonyms. For instance, you can't use *cold* or *sizzling* to spin off from hot, but you could use *Arizona, borscht,* or *miniskirt.*

Play with a friend or by yourself with the help of pencil and paper. Please keep in mind that this is not a competition. Everyone who finds creative spin-off answers really comes up a winner. The goal is to open yourself to all the alternate possibilities.

Playing games like charades or Pictionary, or working crossword puzzles and other brainteasers all stir the creative juices, too, and make your mind more nimble.

To play charades, divide a group into two teams. Have one team decide on a word or phrase or book title (maple syrup, "come hell or high water," Mother Goose) while the other team chooses one member to be "it." After the phrase is given privately to the person who is it, that person must pantomime the phrase to his or her team-mates by using images and gestures to convey syllables or words. Then, switch teams. Pictionary works the same way, except instead of pantomiming the word or phrase, the person who is it draws pictures that symbolize the word.

EXERCISE 45: FRACTURED PROVERBS

A first grade class was once given the first half of well-known, though not to them, proverbs and asked to make up the endings. They came up with "fractured proverbs" like "You can lead a horse to water—but you can't lead him to fire." And, "All's fair in love—and Califor-nia." And, "A penny saved—isn't worth any-thing. You can't buy anything with a penny." The reason the results are so fresh and oddly true is that these kids were not burdened with any established answers. They simply went with what felt right.

Try fracturing some proverbs yourself to build up your own natural alternate thinking power. Alone or with a partner, make a list of the first half of your favorite proverbs or quota-tions and fill in new second halves. See how freewheeling you can be, and make sure to share the results with your partner, or with an appreciative friend.

Just to get you started, here are some beginning phrases you can creatively finish for yourself:

"A stitch in time . . ."
"A fool and his money . . ."
"We have nothing to fear but . . ."
"Give me liberty or . . ."
"If I only have one life to live . . ."

EXERCISE 46: LIKENINGS

This exercise will help open your mind to new
creative ideas. It could be used to help loosen
you up before working on any creative project—from an office assignment to a letter,
paper, or proposal you're trying to write.

Create an evocative one-line situation, such
as, "a day in the park" or "rain on my face."
Then add the words "is like" and follow that
with a statement or an image that seems to fit.
Come up with all sorts of different compari-
sons, or "likenings," for each one-liner, as in the
following example. "Rain on my face is like
. . . the breath of an angel. Rain on my face is
like . . . a new idea insisting it be let in. Rain on
my face is like . . . a gentle joke on me." Once
again, let yourself go. The sky is the limit. If
your mind draws a blank when you try to come

up with workable likenings, try these out for starters:

Sand beneath my feet is like . . .
Children's laughter is like . . .
Having a great book to read is like . . .
Working on a rainy morning is like . . .

"JUMP STARTING" THE RIGHT BRAIN

The "Breath Charge" exercise from Chapter 2 will help you access your creativity on a regular basis if you use it every morning. But in a pinch, hold your right nostril closed and breathe deeply several times through your left to give yourself an extra shot of right hemisphere input.

You can also initiate right-brain activity through sound. Sometimes, when we're faced with a particularly challenging problem or creative task, we instinctively sigh. There are many more refined versions of channel-clearing sound initiators, such as the universal mantra *om*, Tibetan bells, or wind chimes.

For most of us, though, using these options would be highly impractical during the course of a busy day. So let yourself sigh *consciously*, knowing that instead of emitting a resigned sense of frustration, you're signaling your creative self to get going.

. . .

CREATIVITY *IS* THE FLOW

Once you apply uncommon sense to creative problem solving, you'll find you're no longer worried about whether or not you have any ideas, but rather about which of your many ideas you can readily use. Just like intuitive information, some creative ideas will show up in fragments first. Others will come to you more fully, but won't yet be ripe for the picking.

Trust is just as key to developing creativity as it is to developing uncommon sense. The worst thing you can do is dismiss an idea because it seems crazy—the craziest ideas often turn out to be the most workable, simply because they're the most imaginative.

Keep reminding yourself of this, and remember to keep logging your ideas. (You might even want to create your own creativity log; see Appendix.) The right brain is not a memorizer. That's strictly a left-brain occupation, as anyone who has had a brilliant idea in the middle of the night and completely forgotten it by morning surely can attest.

You'll soon determine your own best method for collecting and saving your bits and pieces of creative genius for future reference, but notebooks, including a special notebook next to your bed, tape recorders, index cards, and even scraps of paper thrown into shoe boxes are all popular, flexible methods. Remember to keep looking for patterns as you log down your thoughts, just as you do when you're developing your intuitive messages.

Chances are, if it keeps coming up, it's something worth developing further.

Automatic writing, the process of letting words flow spontaneously onto paper, is an easy and enjoyable method of connecting with the never-ending flow of creative ideas. Everyone from French poets to famous psychics to creative writing students have been inspired by it at one time or another. Here's the uncommon sense version.

EXERCISE 47: AUTOMATIC WRITING

Pick a subject you want to explore—your family, your job, or an actual project you're working on.

To warm up for this creative process, try breathing exercises and neck rolls. Have a pad or notebook and your favorite pen at hand, or use your typewriter.

When you feel relaxed and focused, affirm your never-ending connection to all the information contained within the creative source. I usually begin by saying or thinking something like, "I now open myself to all the creativity I need."

Then just start writing quickly and spontaneously, without worrying about whether the output is smart or "good" or even grammatical. Just let yourself flow with your pen and see what comes up. Later, look for patterns, or significant fragments.

An oral version of the same exercise is not unlike "talking it out." Get a tape recorder. Follow the same procedure, but instead of writing, just let yourself babble on. This is especially good if you've got one of those minirecorders you can carry around with you.

CREATIVE DREAMING

Dreams are your ongoing flow experience. You're quite likely to be at your most creative right after you wake up from dreaming because that's when you're closest to the natural flow state. Look for clues, cues, messages, and ideas in your dreams. Log them in along with everything else. Pay special attention to the ideas you get when you wake up in the morning or in the middle of the night.

Sting, for example, wrote the song "Every Breath You Take" in a single stroke upon waking up with an inspiration in the middle of the night. An advertising executive I know got an idea about a new product for a major corporate client just after waking up in the morning. When she mentioned her idea to the account supervisor, he was astounded: The client was at that moment thinking of adding exactly the same product to their line. You can also solve problems creatively through your dreams.

EXERCISE 48: DREAM PROBLEM SOLVING

Go to bed or take a nap with the conscious intent to come up with a solution. Try drinking half a glass of water, affirming your intent by saying, for example, "I now open to the perfect solution of this problem." When you wake up, immediately drink the water that's left in the glass, and flash on your answer using the white screen technique and referring to the Visual/Feeling Checklist.

You may get a complete answer at that moment, or a fragment you can develop over time. The answer may come later that day or week. You may need to repeat the process, to get a clearer answer. This is one of those exercises that work much better for some people than for others, so don't worry if it doesn't work for you.

CREATIVE CYCLES

As you concentrate and focus, you'll also want to tell your right brain how *long* you'll be creating. Research has shown that the brain seems to work at peak creativity for ninety-minute cycles, so you may find ninety-minute creative periods help you work at your best. But you may also find you have a personal creative cycle or an optimal creative time of day. I personally prefer to sit down for a long period of time, but I take frequent breaks during that extended period. Some people can work at their peak for four hours; others work very quickly and intensely for one.

Once you discover your own personal work pattern, stick with it and try to build your schedule around it as much as possible. It sounds obvious, but many people worry they "should" be creating a certain way. If you work at peak productivity for the two hours right before sunrise, do it! Get ready to dig in your heels if you find, as a stylist friend found, you have long two-week creative cycles that alternate with two-week fallow periods.

We all know some people who are early birds, and others who are inveterate night owls. They simply already know and respect their creative rhythms. Cycles are also known to change, so try to go with the flow if you find that your once up-'n'-at-'em morning peaks turn to after-the-late-show creative highs.

CREATIVE FILL-OUT

Creative ideas often come to us in fragments—just like other uncommon sense information. Applying the Visual/Feeling Checklist and white screen techniques will also help you to expand on your creative flashes. These tools help you decide which of many ideas to go with, and boost your inspiration or focus as you go about executing a creative project.

When he is trying to decide which among many creative ideas from a brainstorming session is best, my husband white screens each possibility to see which idea, as it develops and plays in the movie of his mind, seems the most full, detailed, and workable. He describes it as seeing which image literally has "the most future."

I know a photographer who talks about getting an "escalator" of ideas while he executes a project. For instance, first he will envision a model for a proposed shoot (stair 1). Once the model is literally in the "frame" of his mind, he'll see what she should be wearing (stair 2). Then, with that physical image in front of him, he'll fill in the background atmosphere (stair 3), and so on, until he comes to the top of the stairs—a richly detailed and imaginative uncommon sense whole picture.

Picture your own ideas on your mind-movie-screen. See what images seem to fill out more naturally to discover which ideas really have more life. Then talk through those pictures to develop them even further. Even as you're creating, the picture can evolve, filling in with ever-richer ideas and information.

You can also picture the future of a creative idea the way you picture the future of an everyday situation. Just flash forward a week, a month, or six months with the help of your inner white screen, visualizing a calendar or the changing seasons if you have to. Then use that information to make decisions or gain focus in the present.

LOCATE THE ESSENCE; FIND THE FEELING

The ability to tune in to feelings will aid your creative work as much as it sparks your intuition. Emotion is at the heart of an idea, and it's also what usually communicates that idea to others. Think of the movies, where a tone or a feeling is often the force that really tells or sells the story. Consider French Impressionist painting, which was motivated not so much by a feeling as a concept: a revolutionary new method of interpreting light. Still, when you see a finished Impressionist painting, your response to its beauty is probably an emotional one. In other words, you've felt the *essence.*

Anything you do creatively has its own essential feeling. Finding that feeling is often the key to releasing the full potential of a project. So when you're getting new ideas and trying to tune in to them to see if and how they could be developed, always ask yourself, "What is the main thing I am feeling?" just as you do when you use the Visual/Feeling Checklist.

Locating the essential feeling is also a good way to salvage an idea that isn't quite right. Before you automatically discard a creative approach that didn't pan out, ask yourself if there isn't really a spark, an essence, or a feeling in the idea that is worth saving. When you have that essence, work it in with new creative ideas, or put it back in your sandbox of creative bits and pieces to rework at a later time.

The following easy-to-practice exercise will develop your ability to hone in on essential feelings.

EXERCISE 49: GOING FOR THE ESSENCE/ FINDING THE FEELING

Remember this party game question: "If you were a tree, what tree would you be?" Well, it's really just a variation of this next creative exercise. Not as silly as it sounds, it helps you to think in nonlinear terms and, more specifically, to think in a way that quickly reveals the heart of the matter. Both Part I and Part II will greatly help you develop your ability to locate your feelings when you evaluate your own ideas. The more you practice, the better and more confident you'll become.

PART I: QUINTESSENCES. You can do this exercise on your own or in a group. Either way, start by picking a broad category of things that contain a lot of different members: trees, movie stars, birds, flowers, cartoon characters, musical instruments, books, or even pastries.

Then consider each member of your group (or a group of people you know, such as family, office companions, friends, or roommates if you're working alone) either by putting each in turn on your white screen, or spontaneously and literally, from the top of your head, assigning your subject the category member that seems to best express that person's essence.

For example, if your category is pastries, a rather thin and proper friend might suddenly become a cheese straw. If your category is musical instruments, that majestic-looking teacher with the great voice might become a violincello. Have fun with this, and try not to think at all while in the process. Later you can analyze why, for example, such "species" as Bucky Beaver, an elm tree, and a skylark are the quintessences of your boss.

PART II: FEELINGS. In this variation you will associate an essential feeling with an object or a person, or vice versa. Pick an essential feeling (happy, sad, tired, cold, hot, etc.) and, following the quintessential technique, match that feeling with a person or with a member of a category. What flower best expresses "sad" to you? What tree, "tired"? For people, choose strangers when you're standing in line, dining out, or in a park, and locate their essential feeling.

Note: Choosing friends probably won't provide you with enough creative stretch because you are most likely already fairly aware of their feelings.

EMPATHY IS CARRYING FEELING A STEP FURTHER

Sometimes you can actually personalize a problem to solve it creatively. Remember, when you're in the flow you're in a state of oneness. This creates a powerful empathy that you can apply to creative assignments. When you wholly empathize with a particular problem or challenge, you can feel, from the inside, what it takes to solve it.

Advertising has made a science out of understanding products and consumers by creating personality profiles of both. If you write, *be* your characters. See how you would feel if you, yourself, were each of them in a given situation. If you're writing or talking to someone, try to empathize to the point at which you can really feel what they're feeling. Is your audience reacting to what you're saying? What does he or she need to hear?

Whether you're gardening, cooking, writing, organizing your office, taking a photograph, or working with any other kind of creative project, you can tune in to find out what your project needs. A TV director friend has such a finely developed sense of empathy, he is constantly saying, "The camera wants to be here." There will be more on how to explore the gold mine of this technique to improve your success and prosperity in the next chapter. For now, you can adapt this concept to your particular creative projects. Follow the next exercise to help you develop and use your own creative empathy.

EXERCISE 50: THE EMPATHY CONNECTION

Use the white screen technique to focus in on the person, product, or problem, in order to find a creative solution. See the object of your interest on the screen in full and living detail. Then put *yourself* up on the screen, actually becoming what you're picturing.

It may help to see yourself superimposed over the other image until you meld together, and become one. Perhaps you find you don't need to see yourself on the picture so much as to send your full awareness to the image of the project, and feel that awareness literally entering your subject.

Let's say you're trying to come up with a creative idea, and then a creative plan to sell it. Take turns becoming both the problem (say a shoe that needs to be comfortable but stylish) and your target consumer (who needs to be comfortably styled). If there's a middleman involved (say a manufacturer or an investor) use the technique to empathize with his or her needs, too.

Once you feel you're there in terms of becoming one with your subject, ask your larger self, "How do I feel?" "What do I need?" Pay special attention to visualization and feeling as you tune in to your own responses.

For a truly enlightened creative solution, try problem solving with a variation of the technique just described. See yourself on the white screen as your favorite role model, the one most appropriate for solving the problem at hand. Your chosen role model could be anyone, from your mother or mentor to a great leader, artist or scientist. Then ask your role model/self what to do in this particular situation. If you're the sort of person who sees all sides of a situation, try choosing a very decisive role model for balance. And if you're more of a black-or-white person, choose a model who you think would have empathy with everyone involved.

TALKING IT OUT

Once you've gotten creative ideas, or are in the process of developing them, it's good to talk them out. Conversation itself is a form of the flow. When I'm writing, I often find myself deep in conversation with myself, talking out and talking over different creative options.

Here's a technique that will help you release and loosen your creative muscles. This exercise is especially good for filling in the details of any abstract concepts and is useful in many creative situations, from writing an essay or speech to creating and selling a product.

EXERCISE 51: FREE-FORM FREE-FOR-ALL

Brainstorm to come up with three words that describe the essence of your idea, the feelings that best describe it, or the feeling you want it to convey.

Using pen and paper as your own personal Etch-a-Sketch, take each of the three words in turn and create a flow of associative word leaps.

For example, in one of my business workshops we created a make-believe product called Fruit Chewies. Then we used this technique to establish essential ideas to put toward a way to creatively market it. The three words the group came up with were *fruit, chewy,* and *fun.*

For *fruit* my workshop's examples included "fresh," "natural," and "tasty." For *fun,* we got "joke," "giggling," "laughter," and "bouncy." Don't worry about whether the words make sense—for instance, we got the word "dentures" for chewy. Just let the words and associations flow.

When you've explored all possibilities, look at the words on the screen of your white paper and see what kind of whole picture you've got, or can get. Perhaps you can make more associations from this picture, or create a meaningful story by putting certain words together. Tune in to your inner white screen to see if you can develop the picture even further and to see if certain ideas feel right. You'll probably come up with some interesting concepts, and maybe a surprising answer. You could suddenly visualize the essence of your project, or at least gather enough information to go on and finally solve it.

FOLLOW-THROUGH: UNBLOCKING AND PERSISTING

In order to be fully creative, we often need to have a burning desire. New York artist Mary Boochever says, "My ideas spring from necessity." Songwriter Doc Pomus says, "Why does anyone write? Because they have to." Unfortunately, we all don't have that burning drive to draw on every time we must create. Often, necessities are not self-imposed: We have a deadline to be met, or a client or friend who needs a creative solution—now! Or perhaps we have the time to create, but are in need of a creative energy boost to completely carry through our ideas. Here is an exercise you can use to unblock your own creativity flow and muster up that feeling on demand.

EXERCISE 52: FIRE IN THE BELLY

Sitting with your back straight as you did in the energy-balancing exercise, imagine a great warmth at the base of your spine. Feel that warmth fill your abdominal region, moving up until it fills your entire stomach with its radiating glow.

Now run that fire up through your spinal column in whatever color it shows itself to you—perhaps a white light, or a deep red flame—without worrying about focusing on the colors of each individual energy center along the way. Simply see and feel your spinal column as a long, firm, glowing column of heat.

Finally send the energy upward and outward through the top of your head.

The original creative unblocking force is the flow itself. Whenever you're feeling stuck, try the following tricks to help you get into the creative flow and be reminded of its constant presence.

FOLLOWING THE FLOW OF WATER. Water has long been the symbol and conduit of the flow. Try to consciously use water as a creative stimulant. Drink lots of water to help get your creative juices flowing again. Take a peaceful pause by a fountain, pond, or riverbank if you can for creative refreshment. But in lieu of that, simply go wash your hands. Silly as it sounds, it really helps.

Take advantage of a most natural mundane activity to gain a literal shower of ideas. As you jump into the shower or take a soothing bath, see what ideas or germs of ideas come to you as the water stimulates your senses.

After you towel off, write down anything that came to you, even if it seems incidental. Many times you will find yourself receiving the seed of a creative breakthrough.

FOLLOWING THE FLOW OF MUSIC. Mystery fans will remember that whenever Sherlock Holmes was on the verge of breaking a case, he'd whisk Watson off to a concert, or run off to one himself. Listening to the music, Holmes let his mind flow, and in the process he'd subconsciously pull all his clues together into one seamless, highly creative, and wholly singular solution. Elementary! Try giving *your* left brain up for a moment to the powerful flow of music. Put something highly melodic on the stereo or tape player, and let creative inspiration take over.

LETTING GO

Letting go, like releasing so that you can whole focus, is a very important part of the creative process. In order for creativity to be actively expressed, it must be passively received and accepted by you. When you completely let go, you allow the process itself to regenerate you so you can nourish and harvest new ideas.

You've probably already experienced this yourself if you've ever spent time straining and straining to solve a creative problem, only to have the solution percolate into your awareness after you've finally given in to the urge for a break or nap. We've already seen how dreams, another instinctual method of letting go, are a tremendous source of information. That's why we get so many ideas right after we wake up, or come out of a daydreaming session. Often ideas leap to mind when we're thinking of nothing at all.

In this sense, letting go is as much the first step of the creative process as it is the last. Think of all the new ideas you get when you're thinking about nothing at all. Then think of all the creative techniques you have at your fingertips and all the ways you can use those techniques over time to develop your ideas into fully realized projects.

Relish the luxury of being able to let your ideas bubble up slowly, even as you pay more active attention to what's on the front burner. For instance, an artist friend keeps seeing the image of a certain number hop out onto her mental screen, apparently begging for her to produce a painted rendering of it. She's looking forward to the time when that image will become a literal hot number and be ready to be filled out into a completed work. For now, she's enjoying the leisurely process of letting the picture develop—right before her eyes.

CHAPTER SEVEN

UNCOMMON SUCCESS AND PROSPERITY

YOUR ABUNDANCE CONNECTION

Just as opening to the source of your uncommon sense naturally helps you to more creativity as well as intuition, it can greatly help open you to more overall abundance in your life. In fact, infinite abundance is another name for the riches that flow from the source. Abundance can take the material form of prosperity and success, but its whole picture includes everything from love, time, energy, creativity, and intuition, to a sense of fulfillment—professionally or otherwise. Ultimately, abundance is anything at all you need to support and nourish your whole self as you follow its path through life.

In your inherent source-connection you already have access to everything you need, material and spiritual, to find your life's fulfillment. You also have the innate potential to manifest more and more wealth of every sort in your life, just as you have the ability to increase your intuitive and creative skills to better fulfill your path. The first step toward realizing the full potential of infinite abundance in your life is simply to become aware that you have a natural connection to it. Once you know that, you'll have constant access to its limitless possibilities.

To realize your potential for success and prosperity you need to consciously strengthen and affirm your abundance connection. You'll use the techniques you've already developed—whole focusing, affirming, and visualizing—to more powerfully align yourself with the flow of infinite abundance and get the ball rolling. A healthy attitude—which is neither too greedy nor too needy—is another form of affirmation, and it's a particularly important tool for increasing your own success and prosperity quotient.

The constant awareness of your inherent prosperity will also allow you to reshape the way you are realizing all the success available to you in your life. Remember, as you grow and evolve along the spiral of awareness, your success path and your perception of it will evolve as well. When you feel frustrated, know that you can also tap into your awareness of the infinite flow of abundance, and that, eventually, the tide will turn and abundance will flow your way. Simply affirm your source-connection as you do when you're affirming your uncommon sense, see that you've already achieved your goal, and then let the process of manifesting that goal flow and evolve naturally.

EXERCISE 53: MAKING YOUR ABUNDANCE CONNECTION

Add this exercise to the end of your basic, daily energy-balancing routine whenever you feel the need for an extra-strong abundance connection: on the day you ask for a raise or new responsibilities, while you're brainstorming for that new home business, deciding what option would be the most successful, or trying to make the most of the first few months of an important career move.

First, follow the basic energy-balancing exercise. When you're finished, bring your focus back to the heart energy point. Now breathe into that point, really seeing and feeling the green light radiating there. Continue breathing deeply as that green light strengthens and spreads through the entire area.

When you are ready, affirm, "I now open myself to the endless flow of infinite abundance. Success and prosperity open to me as I open to them and as I need them."

Continue to affirm regularly in both attitude and word, while keeping an eye out for insidious negative affirmations like, "I'm broke," or even, "I can't afford that." You could replace them with a thought such as, "I'm working on it." Know that you *are* working on it—*wherever* you happen to be on your own path to success and prosperity. Whether you're shooting for a new sweater, a new car, or a new corporate acquisition, you're already and always in the process of claiming and evolving your personal abundance.

PUTTING IT ALL TO WORK

As you continue to develop your uncommon sense, ideas for creating more success, prosperity, and abundance will naturally occur to you. You can really put these ideas to the test in the workplace. Doing good, successful business requires far more than knowing and applying facts. Whatever your line of work may be, it can only be enriched, and you can only be made richer, by using uncommon sense to fill in the facts and get a jump on getting the big picture.

We've all seen dramas about street-smart detectives and savvy lawyers who followed their hunches to fill in the blanks before all the facts were uncovered. It's the nature of uncommon sense to provide you with a "vision" before you have the facts or figures to back it all up. So don't dismiss ideas or strategies just because you don't yet have the data to support them. This is something I really stress in my business workshops, where many of those attending are required to think creatively but still "have their butts" on the (bottom) line.

In day-to-day business dealings, there's a tendency to take only the most logical steps instead of allowing for some powerful intuitive leaps. Purely logical minds tend to come to the same kind of logical conclusions, and in the business world, doing the same thing everyone else is doing is a surefire ticket to mediocrity. Creative solutions in any line of work require creative thinking and intuitive leaps of faith.

On a very practical level, going for the intuitive vision first and working backward from that vision to prove its viability is often a whole lot easier and more productive than blindly following logic or hard data. Following logic step by step without a vision of the big picture to guide you can often lead you in the wrong direction and eventually leave you at a dead end.

The "New Coke" debacle of several years back is a great example of what can happen when you try to navigate the route to success without the benefit of uncommon sense. New Coke was hatched after the Coca-Cola Company's expert research "proved" consumers clearly preferred a sweeter cola in a series of blind taste tests. Those hard facts, however, were not interpreted within the bigger, less quantifiable picture of Coca-Cola's special appeal to the American consumer over the years. It was a classic case of businesspeople blindly following their sense of logic without the added vision of their uncommon sense.

A look at the way the decision was made will demonstrate the importance of failing to see the big picture. The new product was tested by giving passersby small Dixie cups of two unnamed colas—one sweeter than the other. The tasters had no idea what they were tasting, so the only conclusion that could have been made from specific research was that consumers simply preferred a sweeter tasting cola. The company failed to tune into the uncommon essence of Coca Cola itself. On a primal, non-rational level, Coke isn't just a drink, it's an American institution.

The result? New Coke was launched, was a financial and PR disaster, and "old" Coke was eventually revived as "Classic Coke." If the facts and figures that their research had relied on had been weighed along with the intangible elements that uncommon sense would have revealed, the company may very well have come up with a more inspired solution to increase their overall market share. Remember, uncommon sense thinking is *whole* thinking. It solves business problems by seeing them in a broader perspective, in which *many* solutions are possible, including solutions that might never have been revealed by following logic alone.

When you make business decisions based largely or

even partly on your uncommon sense, you'll find that you naturally keep closer tabs on the ways in which those decisions play out. This instinct will naturally give you the opportunity to make adjustments in your uncommon sense decisions by going with the flow and righting the course of your vision with your common sense. As the right brain leads the way, this give and take between the left and right hemispheres will guide you toward the absolutely best solution based on both approaches to the problem.

Remember, business projects tend to develop over a period of time. Whenever a consensus is required, very little is instantaneous. The direction of the flow, however, can change suddenly midstream. In cases like these, your uncommon sense will always give you a jump on the competition and help you avoid very practical, bottom-line-oriented pitfalls way before the facts and figures would indicate a problem is coming up. Your reward will be a reputation for business savvy, good instincts, and creative problem solving.

On the other hand, if hard reasoning and research is your bread and butter, you don't have to completely forgo the help of your uncommon sense: Just reverse the process and let the left brain lead the right. A product researcher I know uses his intuitive and creative thinking to make more sense of the numbers that he's getting. Numbers are subject to interpretation, and uncommon sense is the key to more deeply integrating and understanding hard data.

Many prestigious figures in the business world made it

to the top by going with uncommon sense despite the figures. Fred Silverman, the former NBC-TV president known as "The Man with the Golden Gut," is famous for going with his intuition and against research. This kind of uncommon sense in programming has helped keep shows on the air that didn't research well, including major successes like *All in the Family* and *The Mary Tyler Moore Show.*

As president of RCA, Jack Chamberlain also had to rely on his intuition to decide whether to go with eight-track or audiocassette tapes. His hunch told him to go with cassettes, even though eight-track had better fidelity, and the rest is history. A recent study has shown that CEOs of major companies use their intuition in 80 percent of all decisions they make. So why not you?

No one is advocating that you throw caution to the winds and act only on your gut, but unless you use your instincts too, you won't have all the very helpful details of the big picture at your disposal. Psychologists have pointed out that there is a correlation between entering high risk/high finance fields and being open to intuitive guidance. In such ventures, one must come to expect the unexpected, and try to see ahead as far as possible to take advantage of trends. Maybe that's why so many achievers in so many risky areas from Wall Street to politics, show business, fine arts, advertising, and sports take advantage of the information a good psychic or astrologer can offer them. Every year I see a greater percentage of these "success types" myself in my private practice and uncommon sense workshops.

To steadily increase your own intuitive business instincts and overall prosperity quotient, just keep following the flow, practice your uncommon sense exercises as regularly as you can, and check in with your larger self for confirmation as you go along. Developing your uncommon sense skills in general will enable you to more clearly tune in to that sometimes subtle confirmation process, and help you make the very best business moves and decisions.

For more specific ways to tap into the flow of uncommon sense and develop some uncommon success, read on. Use both your common and uncommon sense to see what best applies to your own field and how to use it. Then get ready for opening to uncommonly successful guidance of your very own.

SELLING WITH EMPATHY

We're all involved in selling at one time or another, whether it's selling an idea, getting a point across, selling ourselves to a prospective employer, or actually holding down a sales position. In any of these situations, your uncommon sense can go a long way toward helping you to accomplish your goal.

A story about my father-in-law will show you just what I mean. The man was what is commonly known as a "born salesman." He sold so many storm windows during the housing boom of the sixties that he had to move his business to another county to find people he hadn't already sold to. He was so well known in the last town he settled in, he was called its unofficial mayor. The secret of his success was the very caring way he had of intuiting and filling his clients' needs.

Just as he had an instinct for knowing when to close a sale, he also had a knack for knowing just how much his customers could afford. He often found himself "unselling" certain customers on some more expensive features, costing himself initially on commissions, but creating an invaluable reputation for himself as an honest businessman. His intuitive sales approach paid off handsomely as his grateful customers referred scores of new customers, who he treated in the same caring fashion.

Having empathy for a client's needs helps to strike a balance between buyer and seller, and also helps to find the sales solution inherent in the sales problem. Inevitably, the better salesperson is the one who's most caring. The winning sale is made by going with the flow of the situation. In that flow you can intuit a client's needs and know when to press on, when to back off, when to try another approach, and when to close the deal.

A boutique owner friend of mine adds creativity to that blend. Whenever I visit her store, I find her making truly inspired suggestions to her customers about how to creatively adapt or even alter the clothing she sells to fill many needs. One day when I complimented her about this, she said, "Oh, when I come to the shop I just turn on the program." In other words, she instinctively affirms to herself that she'll go with the flow to help her customers make inspired choices, and help herself make some wonderful sales.

Marketing is another aspect of sales that requires good instincts and the ability to empathize with the consumer. Ken Hakuta, also known as Dr. Fad, has an uncanny ability to take offbeat products and turn them into overnight success stories. Hakuta specializes in finding items people don't need but are going to fall in love with anyway, like Wacky Wallwalkers, those charming little plastic creatures that crawl up and down your walls by themselves. Hakuta was introduced to the critters when he opened a package from Japan a few years back. He didn't need consumer research to tell him he had a hit on his hands. He just knew it.

The secret of Hakuta's success lies in the fun he has with his work and his terrific knack, or empathy, for knowing which items people are going to go mad for. You, too, can use empathy to help you come up with the best business ideas and solutions.

EXERCISE 54: THE EMPATHY CONNECTION

Next time you need to create or market a product, devise an organizational system, write a presentation, or fill another kind of business need, try imagining that you *are* that end product or goal. Find out what *it* needs. You've probably already used this technique whenever you've said to yourself while in the process of working out any problem, from decorating a room, to writing a paper or presentation, "It *needs* something . . ." You've definitely used it if you tried the empathy exercise in Chapter 6.

First, breathe deeply, and see the white screen form in your mind's eye. Sometimes it helps to start by seeing the project you're working on, and to then picture yourself superimposed over it, literally fusing and becoming one with the task at hand. Or after getting the picture of that project on your screen, breathe into both that image and your third eye energy center. This will fuse the two together and allow you to get a mind's eye view of your project's personality and needs.

If you are dealing with a product, *be* that product and try sensing both your needs and how you fit into your consumers' needs. If the product is used on a part of the body, be that body part. If you are devising a new filing system or computer program, be that system and sense what you need to function smoothly and efficiently. If you're preparing a presentation, use the empathy system to feel what tone or wording you yourself need to get your point across. This technique can be applied to people, too. What does your client need? Your boss? Your organization? Find out by using your uncommon sense to be that person or structure.

In the very early 1970s the company that made Arm & Hammer products asked their advertising agency to develop a name and image for their new nonpolluting laundry detergent. Although similar products sported bold graphics and cutesy names like "Ecolo-g," the young creative executive on the account used his uncommon sense to really put himself into the box and to identify with the product on a very primal level.

As the product, he felt that to fulfill his needs he needed to go against the tide of accepted detergent imagery. In fact, he felt he needed a definitely less-than-flashy name and a package that looked like the old Arm & Hammer baking soda box—which consumers had always associated with simplicity and purity. His co-workers considered the idea half-baked since it defied conventional "detergent thinking," and would probably confuse consumers. Fortunately, the agency president was more of an intuitive type himself, and recommended the "simple solution" to the client—whose product is still encased in a package that looks like a big box of baking soda and is the only one of its original competitors still around today.

LITTLE VOICES, LITTLE FLASHES, LITTLE FEELINGS

Developing the ability to follow our little flashes, little voices, and little feelings can certainly help us on the job.

Eloise, a personnel director, says she's always using her uncommon sense to read between the lines of the résumés she receives. Once she found a job applicant who looked perfect on paper, but something told her he just wouldn't work out. She passed along this information, but it went unheeded. The candidate was hired, and a few months later he got the company in trouble, costing them a lot of time and money.

Eloise's uncommon sense also helps her to discover perfect candidates even when their credentials are less than perfect. As a result, Eloise has got a great track record for filling positions with the right people as she follows and develops her flashes of insight and strong gut feelings.

Dick, a brand manager, was in charge of renting a car to get his team to a big meeting. The rental company said everything was fine, but Dick had a gnawing feeling he should change his plans and get to the lot no later than twelve noon even though the car wasn't needed until somewhat later in the day. Not used to having such a strong feeling, Dick acted on it, and ended up renting the very last car on the lot. As a result of that successful uncommon sense experience, Dick has started to trust and follow his hunches a lot more often than he used to, with very beneficial results.

.   .   .

REVELING IN THE OBVIOUS; "STUMBLING" ON
THE LESS THAN OBVIOUS

A schoolteacher client of mine found she had a knack for buying houses that quadrupled in value over a very short period of time. She describes it as just getting a "sense" of their potential, and finds the process quite obvious.

Uncommon sense can be so natural, it indeed feels obvious, which may only be the effect of the irrefutable power of uncommon sense. Entire fortunes have been made by people following the "obvious" directions, and making the "obvious" decisions with the "obvious" clarity of their own inner sensing.

Sometimes, your uncommon sense may also see you through a situation that seems less than obvious. Dorothy, a literary agent, was contacted by a team of authors who were offering what she felt to be a very timely project. These authors only had a limited amount of time to see many different agents. Normally a very deliberate person, Dorothy suddenly found herself cancelling a whole day of appointments to meet with them on the basis of a strong hunch. Even when they called and told her they'd gone with another agent, she was confident she hadn't heard the end of it. Sure enough, a few days later, the authors called back to say they'd decided to go with her after all.

Whatever your business decision, obvious or otherwise, your uncommon sense will help you make the best choice possible. Consciously tap into its power by checking in with your higher self, following the Visual/Feeling Checklist, and by using empathy to get that literal inside track.

(UNCOMMON) TIMING IS EVERYTHING

Good timing is an absolutely wonderful business benefit of being in the flow of uncommon sense. Dorothy sensed the timing was right for her book project. I recently heard a story about Clint Eastwood having a psychic timing experience while he was shooting the film *Pale Rider.*

Eastwood had carefully worked out a filming schedule to include a sequence of some dying autumn leaves that would open his film but would be shot later on in the schedule. Yet suddenly he woke up one morning and decided to shoot the dying leaves that day in place of another scene. So at great potential cost and inconvenience to all concerned, the lineup was changed and that sequence was completed. When the cast and crew woke up the morning after doing so, every tree was absolutely bare—every last leaf had fallen during the night. Eastwood's unsettling and seemingly oddly timed schedule change had suddenly saved the day, and a very important part of his film.

As a director, Eastwood is famous for going with his intuition. During production, he changes schedules constantly. Yet his pictures always come in on time and on budget. He has said, "You have to wait out fate; you can't meet it head on." That really means, of course, that you've got to go with the flow to achieve the most success. When you do, you'll be able to shift your focus as it becomes necessary to maximize opportunities, and be rewarded with the fruits of perfect timing.

YOUR NATURAL FLOW OF COURAGE AND CONFIDENCE

Let's face it: In order to really make it, in the material world or otherwise, it takes plenty of courage and confidence. Being in the flow gives us confidence as we begin to experience an unerring sense of knowing. In turn, we begin to develop courage to keep going forward with the flow. Having courage and confidence together allows us to take the risks we often need to truly realize success. When we're really going with the flow, those courageous leaps of faith somehow don't seem that risky at all.

Take the example of another of Dorothy's clients. This author sent Dorothy and many other agents an unsolicited manuscript. Months later, as Dorothy was straightening her office, she discovered the work hidden under a pile of papers. It was totally battered and covered with dust, but she cleaned it off, took it home to read, and decided she was interested.

When she called the man's office, his secretary immediately said, "He's not here right now, but he said if you called to tell you to just go right ahead with it." Even though the odds were very slim and much time had already passed, the author, with striking certainty, *knew* that Dorothy and Dorothy alone would eventually be the one to successfully represent him.

Your uncommon sense will surely guide you onto your own unique path toward success and prosperity. You know you're in the flow when you suddenly possess the uncanny ability to run across the very resources and information you need. Not only does this phenomenon help you out practically, it also confirms the appropriateness of a chosen project.

I know a graduate student who is writing a dissertation that's a real research challenge. To complete it, he has to constantly use his wits to ferret out very obscure bits of information. As if by chance, or so it seems, he keeps on just running into people who have whole boxes of the specific kinds of papers he needs. This kind of experience reassures him to continue the risky business of this most challenging project.

Sometimes you just get a powerful hunch about a path you should take, but that hunch is very short on the tons of information you think you need to follow it through. Never mind. If a hunch is so strong you can't ignore it, try following it anyway. Many of the most successful careers have been built by those who recognized and could seize a good idea when they got one. For instance, I know a TV producer who felt a persistent desire to go to Chicago, a city where she didn't know a soul. She finally had to act on it, and when she arrived, she quickly connected with a project that was perfect for her talents.

As she started developing it, ideas and favorable circumstances started pouring in, and kept on pouring in, even though she had no tangible resources or contacts in the city. To her, clearly, the signs were right. This pattern confirmed to her that she was on the right track, while it also provided her with a wealth of practical resources.

Courage and confidence seem to come together effortlessly in the phenomenon known as beginner's luck. This type of success results from an unjaded openness to the flow of limitless possibilities. How many times have you heard a story about a smashing success that began with some version of, "I didn't know any better so I just jumped in—and made it!" Adding a burning desire to that open-minded approach can often make beginner's luck close to inevitable.

I know a normally shy, but very competent woman who decided she wanted to do research for a prestigious national news show even though she lacked a media background. New to that world, she was naively oblivious to the odds against her. She wanted the job so badly, that she pulled out all the stops. After sending the show's producer a telegram that extolled her virtues, and a newspaper that headlined the illustrious addition of her talents to the staff, she landed the job for real. One giant step on her success path and one more beginner's luck story for mankind!

No matter where *you* are in terms of your own prosperity or career path, treat each effort you make toward success as a fresh beginning with unlimited potential. You'll release the doubts and hesitations that block your prosperity flow, develop the confidence and courageous risk-taking instincts of an energetic up-and-comer, and open yourself to beginner's luck every step of the way.

Not everyone has that all-consuming, emboldening desire to follow a definite career-related path. Sometimes you may not know what you want, or you may be ambivalent about which of several paths to take. In these situations, get support from the fire in the belly technique you learned in Chapter 6, which will provide you with courage for creative risk taking in your professional life, and help you to see your unique career path as it lifts you into the flow.

For a special boost, try the next exercise whenever you want information about your path and for helpful guidance along the way.

EXERCISE 55: TUNING INTO YOUR SUCCESS AND CAREER PATH

Do your warm-ups, including energy balancing, breathing, and focusing on a chosen energy point. Put up the white screen as you affirm, "I now open myself to the perfect unfolding of my career path. I open myself to words and feelings that will show me that path now." Keep breathing into your white screen, and see what emerges in words, pictures, or feelings.

Keep checking with your higher self for explanation and further guidance. Are you seeing a complete picture, or a fragment of one to come? Ask for a sense of time. Is there a message concerning direction about the way you should approach your career at the moment? Is there any new idea to develop, or a plan to be put into action, or is your picture showing you what will evolve in the future?

Always ask your higher self how you can apply this information as you develop an overall awareness of your success/career path and plan. In addition, always check in with your higher self for any possible uncommon sense cues when you hear about new investments, peruse the classifieds, and read business books and biographies of illustrious business people.

BEING YOUR LIFE'S ENTREPRENEUR

Entrepreneurs are famous for the sort of courage and determination we've been talking about; that is, the sort of courage that allows them to forge ahead and follow their desires against all odds. Most often, they do so without the security of a fully detailed map to steer by, or seemingly any tangible means with which to manifest their plans.

Consider the success story of two IBM researchers in the 1970s. Like many other scientists of the day, they happened to hear of something called superconductivity, the theoretical possibility that electricity could travel through a ceramic compound without creating any friction or without any loss of energy occurring at all.

At the time, no such ceramic compound had been created, but imagine what the world would be like if power were as unlimited and inexpensive as running water. The implications were, and still are, incredible.

This is exactly what the IBM scientists thought. However, IBM had given express orders *not* to pursue this endeavor, which they thought was impossible, practically speaking. The scientists, however, had a strong hunch that the company was wrong this time. That hunch was backed up by the common sense of their scientific training, and it was so compelling that on nothing but a wing and a prayer, they defied company orders and for two years spent every spare minute conducting experiments on ceramic compounds, at great personal inconvenience and professional risk.

Two years later, they made the first crucial discovery about the practical version of the compound their superiors had called impossible, and opened up a whole new branch of the electrical industry at the same time. Today superconductivity is becoming a reality, and those two scientists are now patent holders at the forefront of the industry. So now, not only do they have a very exciting position in this brand-new market, but they also have the satisfaction of having made one of the greatest modern scientific discoveries. Now there's an example of following instincts and getting the abundance flow flowing for our times.

Then there is the story of Ellen, a very successful suburban caterer. When she went to local banks for a start-up loan, they turned her down because of her scanty credit history. She kicked in most of her life savings to get her business started. Although Ellen realized on an intellectual level that she'd put herself in a very risky position, she also began to feel a mounting sense of excitement about the venture. As a result, her intuitive guidance was flowing to her twice as fast. She began to come up with inspired recipes, cost-saving techniques, and clever promotional plans faster than she could write them down. No wonder her first affairs were judged to be a great success!

A few months down the road Ellen was starting to feel even more comfortable with the almost daredevil approach that seemed to be her developing success style. When she realized without question that her business style was to take big risks, Ellen jumped out of the frying pan and into the fire, and decided to go for some important corporate accounts right off the bat. It was an enormous chance to take, and she could have failed miserably. Ellen simply decided to trust her ever-sharpening instinct that she did her best work when she allowed for a good, healthy dose of angst to liven things up.

Things didn't get better right away. One of her first major affairs was a logistical disaster, and she lost the account. However, by the time Ellen began to cater the local Fortune 500 company's client presentations, her courage, determination, and instinctive understanding that she had to do it *her* way began to pay off in spades.

Not only was this particular plum client wild about her, but her reputation spread among the client's corporate luncheon guests, who, one by one, began to request her services themselves.

With little effort Ellen was soon at the helm of a thriving operation that had to turn clients away. In retrospect she realized that if she had played it the safe way and ignored her gut instincts, it could have taken her years and a much larger capital commitment to reach the same position.

If any of these stories ring a bell with you, no matter how faint, that's good. Basically, we should all be entrepreneurs of our own lives, going with the flow and taking charge of our careers with courage, confidence, and self-esteem. No matter what the particulars of your situation may be, always remember that on your path, *you* are the captain of the expedition. Your larger self will help you navigate your life to your greatest abundance, whether your path leads to the reward of being the head of a happy household, or the head of a powerful company.

When you're musing over long-term moves, keep tuning in to your career path to see what patterns and details come up. Like any uncommon sense information, some pictures will seem to have more life than others. Keep on developing them until the time is right, adding common sense to the mix until you come up with an abundance formula any entrepreneur would applaud.

. . .

FLEXIBILITY

By now you've probably gathered that the common thread in all of these success stories is the ability of each person to go with the flow, following his or her uncommon sense even when numbers, schedules, hard data, or popular opinion might indicate otherwise.

Imagine what chaos might have ensued on Clint Eastwood's set if he had stuck with his original schedule, or the opportunities Dorothy and my friend the TV producer might have missed if they had shrugged off their hunches. In the short term, going with the flow can be of great help in your business dealings, but in the long term it will do much more than that—it will really let success and prosperity flow. Many, many long-term successes are built on the ability to sense the way things are flowing, and then to move along with them.

Consider the story of a translator I know. She had an overwhelming intuitive sense that she should travel to Spain directly after graduating from college, even though she didn't know a lick of Spanish. Once there, she found herself taking to the language like a duck to water, sailing her way through an intensive Spanish program, where she heard about a school that hired American English teachers. She really wasn't looking for that sort of thing, but on a whim she went to inquire about the position, and it turned out to be the very day they were hiring for the next semester. Following the flow, a career had suddenly been born. Within months, clients were asking for her to do some translation work, and once back in the States, her uncommon sense led her to more translation opportunities, including a chance meeting that resulted in her work being featured in a prestigious magazine.

All the experiences my friend has had in this "surprise" field have met with great success, and together they help form and keep developing the big picture of her career path. Some of her moves are more spectacular than others, which might just seem like common sense. But you really know you've gotten the knack of applying uncommon sense to your career life, or the rest of your life for that matter, when each move seems to flow naturally into the next, without a lot of fireworks or fuss.

In this sense, there is really no such thing as a detour on your career path. It's all part of the whole. Building your prosperity on a literal wing and a prayer means affirming success in your life, and then going with the flow of your unfolding success path. Just check in with your larger self along the way. Let the flow of your own uncommon sense lead you to investments, clients, jobs, and whole new careers, and help you make the most successful decisions.

It also helps to be aware that you're developing a flexibility that will continue to help you meet and make all choices that come your way as you move along your path. Don't worry about the details—they'll evolve and fill in naturally as you develop your uncommon sense and as your course itself evolves. The fear of details, which I like to call the "what will happen if . . ." syndrome, is very common. Know you *will* have the flexibility and awareness required to deal with those details as they come up, and you'll be that much more able to be open to your own unfolding prosperity/success path.

ABUNDANCE MAGIC

For an extra shot of fun, and a real exercise in the art of being uncommonly open, try applying the following bits of magic, anytime, to transform your current prosperity status and attract more success and wealth.

PYRAMID POWER. Paste the pyramid and eye from the back of a dollar bill onto your wallet. The designers of the dollar bill knew a lot about the deeper meaning of symbols, and that little slip of paper features many images that are absolutely made to affirm abundance. The eye within the pyramid, for example, represents divine abundance manifesting itself in actual physical form. How wonderful to think of every dollar bill as prosperity put into real and ever-increasing action! Fastening that little pyramid onto your wallet can provide an effective visual affirmation and reminder of what you're attracting.

COPPER. Many people unconsciously use copper to attract prosperity by keeping jars of pennies around the house. This common household habit has a dual purpose. Not only does it neatly organize all your pennies in a single location, it also taps into a traditional method of affirming prosperity at the same time. You may be surprised to know that the ancient alchemists routinely placed copper inside glass to "create" gold. Modern science also appreciates the special properties of copper. Its unique physical composition makes it one of the best conductors of electrical energy. It also creates very little resistance to many other kinds of energy as well, which is why chefs prize copper cookware for its ability to heat quickly and evenly.

Is it any wonder that metaphysical wisdom singles out copper as an especially good conduit for prosperity energy? Try keeping jars of pennies around in plain view to make it easier for your own innate abundance to reach you, and to simply remind yourself that you have the "currency" of prosperity at hand. Also try wearing copper jewelry whenever you need a special reminder of your ability to attract more abundance into your life.

GREEN PLANTS. Remember, green is the color of love, prosperity, and growth. In addition to providing fresh oxygen, green plants are said to increase the prosperity vibrations. If you look around a brand-new Chinese restaurant, you'll see that the ancient Chinese custom of blessing new businesses with a lucky green plant survives to this day. Filling your own work or living space with green plants is a great way to affirm prosperity. It may also remind and inspire you to affirm your abundance connection with green light in your daily warm-ups.

FENG SHUI. The Chinese also developed the art of ideal physical placement, or *feng shui*. Originally developed to determine the most beneficial placement for a newly built house—in terms of sunlight, the weather, the landscape, and so on—this art soon flourished and expanded to include the placement of furniture and objects within the home and workplace.

Feng shui advises us to face our desks toward the door of a work space to attract prosperity and abundance. The positioning has to do with best aligning yourself with the energy flow into, out of, and throughout the room. This uncommon advice also contains more than a germ of common sense. Imagine walking down a row of offices. Which sort of person seems more powerful and vibrant to you as you pass by? The sort who is hunched over, facing away from you and toward a blank office wall, or the sort who is ready to greet a visitor head on?

Water is also an important part of the *feng shui* discipline, and any property overlooking water is regarded as being especially powerful. Obviously, not all of us have the opportunity to relocate our offices or homes to follow this advice, but simply keeping a container of water around will ease the way for your prosperity and success just as it eases the way for creativity.

A vase of water nourishing beautiful flowers certainly counts—and the flowers themselves, being green plants, will also affirm prosperity. A bowl of goldfish will help do the trick, as well, and you'll be bringing in another prosperity-inspiring element—the color gold—at the same time. Visions of bullion aside, the golden hue not only helps you to focus on success, but it also helps sharpen and balance your business judgment.

Remember, love is just as much a part of your abundance quotient as financial success and prosperity. It's certainly an area in most of our lives that could use a shot of magic every now and then. See the Appendix for tricks on how to help create and maintain uncommon love.

CHAPTER EIGHT

UNCOMMON ADVICE

As your inner awareness expands, the time may very well come when you feel the urge to broaden or vary your methods of developing your own uncommon sense. Yes, all the answers you ever need are inside of you. From time to time, though, you might want to seek the input of a professional psychic counselor or take instruction from an expert in one of the many psychic arts. This is really just a way to continue the process of developing your own awareness by expanding it with another unique, empathetic, and finely tuned point of view. Since we are all connected, in a manner of speaking, you're merely checking in with another aspect of your larger self. The more you develop your awareness, the more options you'll have. In this chapter I'll discuss some of the choices available to you and explain how they can help.

TO GO OR NOT TO GO . . . TO A PRO

These days, the variety of psychic counselors available to us is exhilarating—and confounding. If you live in an urban area you've probably noticed signs and ads for everything from psychic consultations to psychic fairs, gypsy tea leaf readings, astrological consultations, and even things like psychic energy balancing and psycho/psychic therapy. If you live in a less populous part of the world, no doubt you've heard a story about someone who's gone to see a psychic counselor even if you haven't been exposed to one yourself.

The most important thing to know about psychic counselors is that they're not really all that different from you. They're simply individuals who have made a commitment to develop and use their own uncommon sense to help others. When you go to see any psychic, all you are really doing is boosting your own uncommon sense by getting a dose of a professional's more powerfully developed abilities. The very best psychic counselor is one who truly acts as a catalyst for others' insights. A counseling session can help you to see your present much more clearly, and it can also highlight major upcoming trends in your life so that you can take advantage of them in whatever way you think best.

Perhaps the best motivation for seeing a psychic counselor is for what I like to call a psychic tune-up. Periodically checking in with a pro to heighten your awareness about what's going on in your life can accelerate your own understanding and spiraling growth process. Basic maintenance like this helps you to keep your own uncommon sense equipment in top shape. Refueled and well oiled, you can then go on yourself to handle rough spots or unexpected shifts, and even learn to steer clear of avoidable problems altogether.

You may also feel the urge to pay a visit to a pro when you reach an important crossroad in any of the seven major life experience categories: romance, work, money, creativity, health, family, and spiritual development. If you do experience a significant loss or setback, an advisor can help you expand your understanding of the situation, and counsel you on how to best deal with it. The perspective is unique, but it can also help support the counseling offered by ministers or psychotherapists at such times.

Any reason, no matter how frivolous, can be a valid one for taking advantage of the opportunity to speed your inner growth from without. Remember, though, a professional psychic counselor cannot make life decisions for you, just as a minister or psychotherapist could not. Like the ghosts of Christmas Past, Present, and Future, professional counselors will use their abilities to tell you what they see coming in your life. But don't expect to leave your consultation with all the answers. Hopefully, you *will* leave with invaluable information that can help you tap your own rich vein of awareness and understanding, and that will ultimately lead you to your own best conclusions.

HOW TO PICK YOUR ADVISOR

The very first step in picking a psychic advisor is hearing or seeing that person's name. You might pick a name off a bulletin board or out of a newspaper with the help of your uncommon sense. Or you may read about a psychic in a publication you esteem, or see the name mentioned in a magazine or book interview with a writer you especially admire.

Someone you know and trust may mention a wonderful session he or she has had. If you come across an advisor's name this way, use your uncommon sense to intuit if your friend or acquaintance is someone whose taste is likely to be similar to your own. If so, this is another good first sign that the counselor in question may be one who resonates with your needs. Many of my own clients come to me from personal referrals because they've felt they were more or less in tune with the people who referred them.

Once you have a name you feel comfortable with, the best way to really find out if the advisor is right for you is to give the person a call. Everyone has the right to call and ask about the sort of counseling a psychic offers without feeling obliged to make an appointment. Feel free to ask as many questions as you need. You might start out by asking the counselor about his or her method and specialty. All counselors have specialties, both in the methods they use and in the kind of information they're especially good at providing you with. For instance, the method I use is psychometry. (You read about psychometry in Chapter 5, and I hope you can practice it yourself.) My specialty seems to be providing a large overview. I help clients to see their true path in life, which allows them, in turn, to get at the meaning of the present events in their lives, as well as what the future may hold.

There are almost as many valuable methods of getting intuitive information as there are psychics. The method you opt for should be a fairly accessible one, but don't let it become a deciding factor. It's far more important to concentrate on the vibes you get from the counselors themselves. Trust your own uncommon sense and remember the Hindu saying that advises, "When the student is ready, the teacher appears." My feeling is that you really just need to tune in at the right time, without worrying too much about your methods.

As you talk to the counselor on the phone, try to tune

in further. Ask yourself, "Do I feel comfortable with this person? Do they sound like someone who will understand me and my path? What does their phone style tell me about their counseling style? Are they very professional and clear? Warm and flexible and slightly more informal? Are they especially curt, or brusque, or spacey?" If the person you're talking to is the psychic's representative, the same information applies.

Ask yourself how that style meets your needs, and whether it makes you comfortable. Someone can be the best possible counselor for your best friend, but only so-so for you. It all comes down to what I call personal resonance. Some psychics will warm your heart and spirit, while other, equally competent advisors will leave your awareness out in the cold. So don't be shy about asking questions, and try to really tune in to the answers you get. Use the Visual/Feeling Checklist to fine-tune your reactions.

Use your common sense, too. Do you feel comfortable with the attitude and language of the counselor? Feel free to ask what kind of space the sessions are held in, if it's important to you. Does the counselor work behind a desk in an office, or in a more casual kind of space where you could kick off your shoes if you wanted to? Each of these environments could have an advantage for you, depending on your own responses and tastes.

If you have a particular social or sexual orientation, you may want to find out how a psychic feels about it before making an appointment. Although a counselor doesn't have to share your orientation to do good work for you,

you certainly wouldn't want to go to see a psychic counselor who is homophobic if you are gay, or a psychic who
is only keen on traditional family values if you have a
nontraditional family decision to weigh.

Also, when you call, be sure to ask if you can tape your
session. Remember, the right brain is not a memorizer,
and it's the very hemisphere you're going to be activating
during your reading. You need to really let yourself flow
during a reading, and must not let yourself be distracted
by the worry that you'll forget what you've learned.

Taping is invaluable because it releases you from that
worry. There are some counselors who provide a labeled
tape with your name and the date of session as a normal
part of the service that they offer, but others will ask you
to bring your own. You might also think twice about
seeing any counselor who doesn't allow you to tape.
There may be a psychic out there who does have a very
valid reason for this request. However, there may also be
those who ask their clients not to tape to prevent them
from comparing notes and discovering that they've all
received suspiciously similar readings.

The fee for the session is something else you should
find out during that initial conversation. You can turn to
the guidelines section at the end of the chapter to help you
determine what a fair session fee would be for you.

.   .   .

IN THE BEGINNING . . .

On the day of your appointment, there is some very important preliminary work you can do to make sure you have the most productive session possible.

First, you need to spend some time focusing on what you want to get out of the reading. Many prospective clients ask me on the phone whether they should bring a list of questions with them. My advice is always the same: Really focus on the questions you want answered, whether this means making a physical list or a mental one.

However you want to collect them, it's good to have within easy reach those specific questions you want answered. They will serve as a wonderful focusing point for the session itself. As one of my favorite bits of ancient Chinese wisdom advises, "It furthers one to have somewhere to go." That certainly goes for psychic counseling sessions, where your questions can become the starting point for receiving crucial information.

On the other hand, if you're *too* finite about exactly what question you want to ask and what answer you want to get, you may very well limit the full potential of your session. If you go into a consultation only looking for very specific answers, you'll close yourself off from potentially invaluable information.

Any question is great for getting the session started, but open yourself to answers that could possibly lead to *other* questions. Sometimes clients who come to me quite concerned about finding the perfect mate have only one type of question and answer in mind. They never stop to think that maybe they need to learn more about themselves before they can learn about their future spouses. If you can go with the flow of the session and stay open to potentially new lines of questioning, you could well receive information far more profound and influential than your original questions warranted.

So even as you make that original list, be prepared to flow with the session and the answers you receive. Anything may happen during the course of a reading. An area of your life that is very much in the background may come into the foreground. Or the answers to your questions may be entirely different from what you'd expected them to be, but even more appropriate than the ones you'd originally considered.

It's also essential to do some whole focusing by yourself before you go to your session. You'll be greatly helping yourself to get the most out of your reading by perfectly tuning in to the flow of your upcoming session. This isn't to say that a psychic counselor just throws out whole information, leaving you to interpret as much as if you had to decipher your own whole uncommon sense messages. But the flow of your consultation could, and may, go anywhere, so the more focused and tuned in you are, the more you can follow potential, intuitive leaps from one area to another. The higher your awareness is during your session, the more you'll click with the higher awareness of your counselor, and that, from my experience, yields a much more open and informative consultation.

Some counselors, myself included, even start out each

session with some whole focusing with the client. Here is my routine, which you can use yourself in any quiet place before your session.

EXERCISE 56: PRESESSION WARM-UP

As in whole focusing, breathe in and out deeply three times, really feeling the release as you exhale. It helps to close your eyes for deeper concentration and release.

Now keep breathing rhythmically as you visualize a bright white light circulating through you and around you, literally illuminating you.

Affirm to yourself or aloud, "I now open to infinite knowledge and to the clarity of the information I now need in my life. I allow the information I need to flow to me as it needs to through the person I am seeing. I accept the highest, most loving, and most useful information."

Keep whole focusing for as long as you like before going off to your session.

Also do yourself a favor and don't schedule your appointment with your counselor on a day when you know you're going to be extremely busy. Sometimes you can't always plan to be calm, but do your best to try.

Along similar lines, realize that psychics get tired and frazzled, too. You may even want to ask before making your appointment what time of day your potential advisor is most relaxed and "on." You may not have a choice, but if you do, wouldn't you much rather be getting your guidance from a rested source? (For that one reason, if for no other, don't even think about calling a psychic at 5 A.M. with a burning question.)

OPENING UP AND GETTING DEEP

Some readings are very structured; others are more free-form. Your counselor may have prepared charts and graphs for you based on your name or your birthday. He or she may look at your hands during the course of the reading, consult cards, or hold an object that belongs to you, as I do. Other counselors have no visible tools or don't need any other kind of information to do their work. The only constant is this: When you go to a psychic you're going to see someone who's a specialist in obtaining and interpreting nonlinear information. So the answer you'll eventually get will be translated from the language of uncommon sense. Think of a psychic counselor as a source middle person, tapping into right-brain wealth, inspired by the left-brain question-and-answer process you, the client, initiate.

Some counselors prefer to deliver their information first and then have you ask questions, whereas others prefer a more free-form, conversational reading. Ask your counselor which kind of feedback he or she prefers. Or, as most of my clients do, let your advisor take the lead. Do always make sure you ask all the questions you need to in order to really understand what your counselor has to share with you. The reading is for *you*. Therefore, the most important thing is for you to have as much under-standing as you can when you leave.

Really try to strike a balance between listening care-fully and asking pertinent questions. During an intuitive counseling session, the information is being filtered through a different awareness, but it is still *your* informa-tion and *your* reading.

Don't think if the psychic asks *you* questions that some-how it's cheating. You are not giving yourself away or giving your psychic too much power if you answer needed questions or give out information or confirmation as the session goes on. Use your uncommon sense to tell if your psychic is, indeed, fishing, but generally, your counselor needs to find the same balance between asking and receiving that you do. If you trust that you've already used some uncommon sense to choose your advisor, you'll flow better with the information you're receiving and contribute more to your own session.

Ideally, the whole psychic consultation process gives *you* the ball so you can run with it. Think of your psychic advisor as a catalyst, a professional whose job it is to help you help yourself. What really warms the collective heart of psychics everywhere is to hear from clients that some-thing they were told allowed them to see things in a new way, or let them find their own inner power to make important changes. Speaking for the pros, I can say that kind of thanks gladdens us more than hearing we were right about a future event. One of my clients even told me, "I learned more in one session with you than I did in five years with my shrink." That's perhaps the most rewarding kind of feedback any psychic could hear.

WHAT KINDS OF RESULTS TO EXPECT

Whatever the method, much of intuitive counseling consists of tuning in to the many thoughts, experiences, and insights you already have about a question, and bringing them into clearer focus for you. Think of a photographer who picks out the most telling or interesting image in his or her lens and focuses the whole shot around it, letting everything else fade out a little. As you look at that finished photograph, its focus helps you see what is most important and what is merely background information.

You can look at psychic counseling the same way. What a psychic counselor does, in one way or another, is to find the perfect focus or most important theme of a certain moment in your life. By sharing the present picture with you, the psychic can then intuit upcoming trends—the way the picture of the same scene might look if it were taken in a few months. The counselor is not the photographer, though, *you* are. You're creating the scenes of your life, and a psychic is simply more practiced at seeing them in the most illuminating focus and light.

Since the professional psychic is tuning in to your

picture *now,* you're probably going to be familiar with many of the issues raised. So you might say that, as far as psychic counseling goes, no news is good news. If everything your psychic brings up is news to you, it's a pretty good sign that you're at least a little out of touch with your life.

Your session will probably include a lot of confirmation of the rightness of thoughts, ideas, and feelings that have already crossed your mind at least once. As your counselor confirms what you've envisioned by singling out or acknowledging certain approaches, hunches, and feelings you've already had, the confusing thoughts that have been battling in your mind's foreground will fall into place around your newly confirmed right-focused picture. You'll be able to really concentrate on what's most crucial in your life at this very moment.

Let's take a look at an example. One of my clients, a writer, came to me for a session on her novel in progress. She was close to finishing it, but had suddenly run into an unexpected twist in the writing process. Instead of wrapping itself up neatly at the end, suddenly many different, unexpected endings were presenting themselves to her. In the course of her work sessions, various approaches to this new dilemma had occurred to her, but when she came to me she simply asked me to tune in to see what information I, myself, would receive about her book, and her finishing it.

As I conducted the reading several things came up. First, I sensed she might need to write out all the possible endings and choose the best elements from each. When

I mentioned this she smiled. She explained to me that strategy had crossed her mind, but she had been afraid that it was just a way of procrastinating, or that, worse, it would lead to a dead end. Then more information came through to me about the book. I asked her if she had changed the name of her main character. Again, she smiled. She said she hadn't, but that she had been thinking about it, and had even talked over the possibility with a friend, keeping the option in the back of her mind. But now that I'd mentioned it, she continued, she'd go ahead and do it.

Finally, I got a very strong impression of the essence of the book in progress. When I mentioned it to her, she looked surprised. She said that was certainly part of the book, but an unexpected part, and one that had been troubling her. As it turned out, the fact that I picked up on its strength and relevance confirmed its importance and allowed her to really concentrate on it, brushing away all the distracting doubt and worry.

Confirmation is easy to apply to your life, since, in general, you've already considered the solution before it is confirmed. By enhancing your awareness of a situation, your counselor empowers you to deal with it. If you are already trying to listen to your intuition, you'll probably find yourself saying things like, "Oh, I was feeling that way but I was wondering if that was really happening or if it was just my imagination."

A psychic can also confirm more general feelings that you are having, and transform those feelings into practical information. Take the case of a client of mine who came to see me when he was feeling ambivalent and apathetic about his position at a PR agency, but didn't know what else he felt like doing. When I tuned in, my uncommon sense told me it was really the right time for my client to leave his present position. I was able to tell him I didn't see any future opportunities and challenges in his job.

I confirmed what his uncommon sense was telling him, and provided him with some practical information to boot. I was also able to reassure my client that I didn't see a dramatic ending, such as being fired from his present situation. As he confirmed the larger pieces of the picture that was falling into place, I was able to focus on smaller, more specific details of the issue. In his case, these details had to do with job opportunities. I gave him the name of a specific company to pursue, and the first name of a man he didn't know at the moment, but who might prove helpful to him in the next three to six months.

These specific details were not meant as foregone conclusions. The point was to prepare my client for the opportunities that were going to present themselves to him in the near future. As the reading developed, I confirmed each specific detail I saw with my client to see if it seemed to make sense for him. If it didn't, I'd try a new twist on the same uncommon sense information until we came up with something that was useful to him. You may have tried this yourself in the psychometry exercise in Chapter 5. Certainly other counselors who use different methods can offer practical information that pinpoints and confirms a client's needs and feelings equally well.

Remember, along with confirmation, much of what a psychic illuminates are upcoming trends in your life so that you can take advantage of them. Lurking behind the most specific and practical detail a psychic can suggest is the sure conviction that a personal trend is coming around the next corner.

If you are the slightly nervous type, and we all are from time to time, a psychic consultation can really soothe your nerves about taking the initiative in any area of your life. Anyone becomes more confident when their inclinations are supported by a little evidence.

Of course, confirmation is not always so straightforward. Since it reflects the flow of life itself, psychic counseling is full of twists, turns, and surprises. Your advisor may intuit that the flow is not moving in the direction you'd prefer, and will advise you on how best to turn the circumstances around in your favor.

He or she may also give you a ballpark estimate of how long it will be before certain plans you have begin to bear fruit. We're all trained to think short term, but if we're truly to progress along the spiral of awareness, we also have to think long term. Gaining long-term insight is like developing your vantage point *from* the spiral of awareness—it can really help you see, accept, and get the most out of what's going on right now. Remember, you have free will. Your advisor is only giving you trends based on the current situation. Your knowledge of those trends can help you change the projected picture, and that new picture may very well be the one that accelerates your growth.

While we're on the subject of twists and turns, your psychic counselor could very well sense that the issue you came to consult about is related to yet another life issue. That is to say, fear of leaving your job could have something to do with fear of leaving your parents. Or a lack of trust in one of your children could have something to do with your lack of trust in your own creative or business talent.

There may be something very primal that comes up in your session—for example, an unresolved and resentful relationship with your family—that you realize will never be completely resolved within the structure of a psychic consultation. It may be time for you to go with the flow of working through that situation by contacting a trained psychological therapist.

Don't be surprised if a compassionate psychic makes that kind of suggestion, or recommends any other form of release or therapy, from isolation tanks to meditation to energy-centering massage. The flow is not particular about the methods you use to gain the results you want. There are infinite solutions to any one problem, and getting at the roots of problems psychically, psychologically, physically, or by any other route is just another way of easing your way toward a greater sense of resolution and abundance.

. . .

HOW YOU CAN HELP THE PROCESS

All different kinds of information will probably be part of the flow of uncommon sense your psychic provides for you as he or she tunes in to your questions. Anything from advice on your path through life and personal challenges, to childhood events, names of loved ones, and estimated dates concerning when certain events will take place, can all be part and parcel of a reading.

The way you respond to this information really influences the kind of reading you get. The choice is yours. You can either focus on the straight facts or go to the very heart of any personal problems you have.

Clients are often very impressed by their counselor's ability to come up with names and initials, or to predict mundane events, like leaking pipes. Accuracy like this is very useful if it enables you to trust the deeper, less verifiable insights your counselor shares with you.

However, try not to focus so intensely on this kind of dazzling surface information that you miss out on the more lasting meaning of the counsel being offered to you. It's my belief that information for information's sake does you and your awareness little good. It's how you *apply* that information, or how your counselor can advise you to do so, that does the trick. Always remember to ask, *"What can I learn from this?"*

There is no such thing as a dumb question. A professional psychic counselor is in the business of compassion. During your reading, he or she is only attuned to you and to your awareness. Any kind of personal judgment your advisor may have should be left outside the office door.

You'll also probably be interested in any information your advisor can give you about the timing of certain events in your life. Although once in a while you may happen into someone who's a real time prediction whiz, generally speaking the best time estimate is a ballpark estimate. You can reasonably expect a counselor to advise you that he or she sees an event coming your way within six months. However, don't count on being told that an important event will transpire on March 3, 1993. Or tomorrow. Or next week.

In fact, if you are only able to focus on the exact time and place something is supposed to happen, you may be missing out on a much more significant piece of information. Since time is a continuum, both the past and the future come out of now, and what happens now will definitely shape both past and future events. Simply sitting on your hands and waiting for March 3, 1993, to come down the pike probably won't accomplish much at all.

Don't be surprised if your counselor uses phrases or words that have special, private meanings for you, and which he or she couldn't possibly have known of. For instance, if you are examining a relationship, your counselor may mention a typical phrase your partner uses. Once you've focused on that phrase together, this may open your counselor to shed further light on the feelings or patterns that lie behind it. Or a psychic counselor may suddenly use uncharacteristic language, which turns out to be very revealing, to describe the person in question. In a recent counseling session I found myself describing a client's relative as a "gay blade." As it happened, gayness was both an issue concerning the relative, and an issue my client was trying to deal with. The strange expression that popped out of my mouth, seemingly out of nowhere, actually opened a discussion that my client immediately felt comfortable with. Every psychic counselor has his or her own form of dazzle—this is only one of many. So look forward to receiving forms of confirmation that are often as unexpected and revealing as the results of the session itself.

GOING WITH THE FLOW OF YOUR SESSION

If you are feeling doubt or uncertainty during a session, try to express it in a nonresistant way. It's an unwritten contract that when you come to see a psychic you've accepted that they're psychic. So try not to challenge your counselor on his or her psychic ability, just as you wouldn't challenge a psychological therapist on his or her credentials during a therapy session.

For instance, asking a psychic counselor how many children you have, just to see if they know the answer, isn't helpful to you. You already know how many children you have. But asking your counselor to give you more specific information about a particular problem your youngest child is having is perfectly valid, and quite helpful as well.

If you don't feel a session is working for you, try and go with it anyway. Later on, when you listen to your tape, you may very well find that you get something out of it you didn't understand at the time. This happens to almost everyone at some point. You may even discover that a part of the reading that seemed off was actually right on the money, and that you just weren't aware enough at the time to absorb and understand the information it contained.

Despite all your careful screenings, it's possible you'll have to leave a session while it's still in progress. If a psychic asks you for more money than was mentioned on the phone, get up and walk out. Call the Better Business Bureau while you're at it. A reputable psychic will not ask you for more money. Furthermore, if a psychic starts talking gobbledygook about evil spirits around you, you should make an immediate exit.

HOW TO READ A READING

When the subject of psychic counseling comes up among a group of people, there is sometimes one person who says, "I went to see X, but X can't be a very good psychic because he only told me good things." A variation on this is the one who says, "Y is a terrific psychic. She tells it like it is. She makes me feel really uncomfortable, and that must be good."

How a psychic delivers the reading is an important issue. It's my personal belief that most people focus on the negative side of life much more than on the positive. Instead of seeking the help of a psychic counselor to anticipate and plan for a positive growth experience, many regard counseling sessions as "reports from the front," or bulletins that can alert them about upcoming battles, so that they can duck the bullets and head for the nearest foxhole. Ironically, by keeping that negative reality on their minds they align themselves more closely to it, and can actually end up bringing it into their lives instead of avoiding it.

To correct for this, many psychic counselors, including me, try to help people rediscover their connection to the source, which is without limitation, and therefore capable of manifesting all the success, joy, and contentment one can desire. This doesn't mean we're Pollyannas, either. It simply means that a dedicated psychic advisor feels a certain responsibility to deliver information in a way that is helpful, which generally means showing what good can come out of any situation that's been intuited.

If I see a potentially difficult situation coming up for one of my clients, I don't necessarily view it as a total negative. Instead, I see it, and express it, as a growth opportunity. If a person is already going through a painful experience, they certainly know it. My job is to show them how to use the information they receive to deal with their pain more effectively, avoid future distress if possible, and, in either case, show how they can go on to improve their lives.

Psychics should never let their egos interfere with their work, especially if a client could be hurt. For example, a friend of mine went to see a psychic who seemed to specialize in financial consultation. This consultant told my friend she would never have any financial security, because as soon as she became solvent, something would always happen to relieve her of her funds. As a result, my friend was advised to spend whatever money she had on things she wanted, so that at least she would be relieving herself of funds in a constructive way. Constructive? This advice certainly wasn't! A compassionate psychic advisor who perhaps had picked up similar information wouldn't have presented it in such a way that the client was left with no alternative but to assume her life was a financial disaster.

The moral is to beware of any advice that doesn't leave room for a growth opportunity. Basically, you should be wary of someone who interprets your reality in an absolutely negative or judgmental way, and who offers no chance for self-improvement or the exercise of your own free will.

Be responsible. If you feel as if something's wrong with the way your psychic's handling the situation, don't ignore it. It's well within your rights to say, "Wait a minute. I don't accept that and don't want to be talked to that way." On the other hand, if your counselor flatters you more than the fox flattered the hen, take that flattery with a grain of salt and probe more deeply into the information that's being offered. Finally, if you find your counselor picking up on some good upcoming trends for you in a sensible and grounded way, while also pointing out the occasional area where there's room for growth, just sit back and enjoy the ride.

THE SIMPLE ART OF PSYCHIC MIX AND MATCH

You may go to more than one psychic over time and find they give you conflicting information. This is just one more reason to check in with your own uncommon sense. One of your advisors isn't necessarily wrong, because as we've seen, the picture of your life can change over time, sometimes over a period as short as a week or a month. If one counselor tells you you're going to be a businessperson and another sees you writing poetry, use your own inner resources to look into the whole of what, together, the two psychics have offered you. You may find that none of the information applies to you, or, it may be that everything else about the reading made sense to you except for this one piece of information.

Perhaps, for example, the information referred symbolically to the poetry within you, or to the fact that you should be more businesslike about your career as a poet. Or maybe you'll be happiest as a business executive who writes poetry on the side, or have a thriving career in arts administration. Use your common and uncommon sense to find out. Situations like this one are all the more reason why the state of your awareness, and hence the state of your life, is ultimately up to you.

It's also important to be aware of the phenomenon I call psychic slants. A very talented and compassionate psychic counselor may still have occasional blind spots, or subjects about which information doesn't come through quite as well or as objectively as it does in others. For example, I tell the few clients who ask that I'm simply no good at predicting the outcome of sports events.

As for objectivity, I know of a psychic who sometimes makes overly negative predictions concerning careers. One reason for this may be that her own career is full of fitful starts and stops. Nevertheless, she's quite wonderful with other kinds of advice, and people who consult with her learn to take any predicted career chaos with a grain of salt.

The comparative worldliness of your psychic can also slant or tint information, which you may be required to reinterpret. Just last month, a colleague of mine highly recommended a telephone psychic who works out of her kitchen in California. "This woman's wonderful," my friend said, "and gives uncannily accurate readings. But just keep in mind there may be some corrections you need to make to allow for her frame of reference. You know, she saw me taking a trip to California, when really she was seeing my house in the Mediterranean. She was right on the money about everything—the warm climate, Spanish style, blue-green ocean. But she just assumed it was California because she's never seen the Mediterranean."

Also, the closer you come to areas not related to your

own direct experience (such as past lives and some information offered by trance channels), the harder it's going to be to validate that information. Again, only your own feelings can validate the information you receive. For the sake of an example, let's say you've explored past life therapy because you believe that for you it has either psychological or spiritual benefits.

A specialist in this area focuses in on one lifetime, or more, that seems particularly resonant for you now. Depending on how many times you go to such a specialist, and on whether or not you go to different specialists, you may find yourself getting what appears to be contradictory information. Ask yourself why that information might be coming at this particular time, and what the essence of its message could be.

There's clearly no physical library you can reference to see if this kind of data is right, so check with your larger self to see if it fits, and while you're checking in, ask how you can apply it to better understand and improve your life. For instance, if a counselor believes you were a musician in another lifetime that was cut short, that may help you to understand why you are a musician now. Or if your career choice seems impossible at every turn and you are advised you had a long and happy career in this area in another life, it may be that you simply have no need to repeat the experience.

A final word on the subject of multiple psychics: It's good to be sensitive to the changes in your own flow, which may make you resonate to different methods and specialties at different times. If you do find yourself being disappointed with psychic after psychic, however, you should consider the possibility that maybe you don't know what it is you're looking for. Use the opportunity to take some time to tune in and center yourself *by* yourself. A rule of thumb: *Three* psychics, and that could be pushing it, should really be the limit at any one time to consult on any one issue.

SOME GUIDELINES AND ANSWERS TO COMMONLY ASKED QUESTIONS

There is no American version of the American Medical Association to give accreditation to psychic professionals, although if you feel nervous about hard credentials you might want to check in with a local spiritual society about a counselor you are considering.

Some people prefer to bring a friend along to sit in on their session. If this is your preference, be sure to ask the psychic if that's okay. Some do mind. Unless it's a specified couples session, many psychics often find they are limited in what information they can divulge and feel hindered by the presence of a second person. Also, you yourself may be less focused when a friend is present. Remember, this is your time for *you*.

Please don't assume that just because your counselor gives psychic advice, his or her schedule is nonlinear, too. If you show up late, you may not be able to extend your session to make up for your lateness. And of course, when you're making the appointment, ask how long the session will be.

As far as fees are concerned, basically you need to let your uncommon sense and your location be your guide. In major urban areas, if you're talking about a reading in the five-to-fifty-dollar range, you're probably talking about a reading with some kind of limitation placed on it (five-to-thirty dollars in less urban areas). You may only receive ten to fifteen minutes worth of information, or even not very good information. Or perhaps the counselor in question is not 100 percent terrific, but is very good on certain issues.

Don't assume, however, that the more you pay the better the psychic. Whether an eighty-dollar consultation is twice as good as a forty-dollar reading depends entirely on the quality of the reader. Other factors to consider when tuning in to an appropriate fee are these: the part of town your advisor works out of (high rent affects psychics, too); how "hot" he or she is at the moment (the law of supply and demand works here, as well); and experience (if I had to go for *one* determining factor, this would be it).

The only real rule of thumb here is to make sure you're source-connecting in the best way for you. But a corollary to that rule is, the more expensive the session or the more esoteric the method, the more questions you should ask, both of the prospective counselor and of your larger self, before committing to a session. Ask yourself, "Would the reading have the same value without all the snazzy packaging?"

WRAPPING IT UP

When your session comes to a close, you'll want to feel both a sense of completion and a sense of continuity. There are a few simple ways of making sure you got what you came for and of keeping the avenues open for further communication.

Like many psychic counselors, I'm often asked, "When should I come back?" The answer is, only you can know the answer to that question. You may never have to see a professional again. You may want to come back in a year, or, as I do (yes, psychics do go to other psychics for information), come in for regular tune-ups. If you're going through a lot of changes, you may even want to come back as soon as the following month. Whatever feels right is right.

An unanswered question about something you discussed in your session may percolate up through your awareness a few days after your reading. If you feel confused or incomplete, by all means call the psychic. Many psychics, including me, even make a point of letting clients know this is okay at the end of each session. Certainly try to have respect for a psychic's time, but if you need a little more clarification about something that came up, do give a call.

The best way to take in and get the most out of a reading is to take it in whole, let what needs to stick, stick, and release what doesn't seem appropriate. You may prefer to review your tape to clarify things. You may also want to listen to that tape every now and then to see if something new catches your attention in a way it didn't before. You'll find listening to the tape also helps you to discern patterns of information that can invaluably point to patterns in your life.

Here is a focusing technique that will help you get the most out of your reading after it is completed. Do this exercise *before* you listen to your tape.

EXERCISE 57: POSTSESSION WRAP-UP

Repeat the breathing and white light visualization you learned how to do in the presession warm-up (Exercise 56).

Then affirm to yourself or aloud, "I now allow infinite wisdom and guidance to flow to me through this tape. I know I will learn and use what I need to achieve my greatest growth."

Keep whole focusing for as long as you like before turning on the tape.

Listening to your tape once in a while will also help you develop your own uncommon sense. You're going to be hearing how a pro really works, and you could easily pick up some professional techniques to apply to your own tuning-in process.

AN UNCOMMON CONCLUSION

Now that you've read this book, you've undoubtedly gathered that having—or using—your uncommon sense means a whole lot more than just getting psychic flashes.

In developing your uncommon sense, what you've really been evolving is a highly practical philosophy of life itself. Uncommon sense is whole thinking—and should be applied to your *whole life.* That means you can really use your uncommon sense to explore all the avenues of your life path, ultimately gathering a much larger sense of its context and purpose. With uncommon sense you can put your whole life into perspective and gain a sense of where it is, as well as where it's going.

Remember, though, that uncommon sense isn't an all-purpose magic wand. As your awareness grows, you'll come to keenly realize and accept the paradox that although sometimes the power of your uncommon sense is so great it can seem almost magical, at other times it will simply seem to have vanished. Always keep in mind that uncommon sense, like your personal path, has a unique flow of its own. Try to go with that flow as far as you can when it feels "on" to you. Remember this during those seemingly off times: Uncommon sense is often so subtle and so natural that, blissfully unaware, you may actually be using it as part and parcel of your everyday thinking.

In general, however, you have been consciously learning how to use and apply your uncommon sense. And you'll become more and more familiar with how uncommon sense works for you personally (and how you can make it work for you) as you continue to develop it. For your ongoing inner workout, here's a list of basic do's and don'ts that should enlighten your process and keep you pointed in the right direction.

.　.　.

UNCOMMON SENSE DO'S AND DON'TS

- *Don't* "inflict" your developing uncommon sense on others—don't be a smarty pants and a show-off. This, of course, is no longer a problem with your developing empathy.

- *Do* help others to tap into their own uncommon sense by asking them, "How do *you* feel about this situation (or person, or decision). What does your *gut* say?" This way, you can guide others to experience their *own* uncommon sense without inflicting your particular beliefs and abilities on them.

- *Do* have fun with uncommon sense, *especially* with other people. Humor, we've seen, immediately raises anyone's awareness. Have fun trying out some appropriate uncommon sense routines with friends, family, co-workers, and mates. You'll allow them to find and use their own uncommon sense, further develop your own uncommon sense skills, and have a lot of laughs in the process.

- *Don't* turn uncommon sense into another "should" to hang over your head in life. For example, don't berate yourself because you should be better at it, or you should use it more often.

- *Do* let uncommon sense flow to you as it comes, and let yourself go with that flow as you truly need to. And do let go of that mental tape that tries to tell you otherwise!

- *Don't* try to analyze why your uncommon sense works sometimes and not others, works in different ways, or even why it works at all.

- *Do* understand that by its very definition uncommon sense is really beyond analysis. Enjoy that refreshing angle, and flow *with* your uncommon sense. You'll be surprised at how much you can integrate it into your life in a very commonsense way after you let it all flow—minus the analysis.

- *Don't* consider anything here to be written in stone. This book is really intended to serve as a guideline that shows you how much you, in fact, already know, and how easily you can tune in to and go with the flow of your own life—in the way that's right for *you*.

As you keep going with the flow and cultivate your uncommon sense, you'll naturally develop a sense of wonder toward your own virtually limitless potential. To experience all of the fulfillment our lives truly have to offer, we need to maintain that sense of wonder, and we need to keep exploring every potential of our paths. We each must do this in our own way, of course. But watch a child engrossed in observing the tracery of veins on a new green leaf, and you'll get a sense of exactly the kind of wondrous, exploring attitude you need.

An almost childlike curiosity will allow us a chance for fulfillment, even as we weather some very adult self-questioning. In those times when you are naturally uncertain about making the right decision, use your *uncommon* wonder to show you the possibilities—especially when the answers you seek don't seem black or white.

Sometimes, no matter how much you allow yourself to flow with your life and your uncommon sense, you find yourself caught in an uphill battle or even downright stalled and stuck in difficult situations. Think of these as growing pains which, as the name implies, can accompany many of our most valuable life (and growth) experiences. The pearl needs an irritating grain of sand to manifest its perfect form. You yourself gain perfection and develop your *own* grit when you learn how to grow from each potential life catalyst. Using your uncommon sense to understand and move through each of these growth stimulators, you can gain a greater sense of resolution and find the contentment you can only know after learning such difficult lessons.

Take advantage of your progress along the spiral of awareness and look to the state of fulfillment that exists beyond any current difficulty. Above all, the main rule of thumb is the same as the one you go by in developing any aspect of your uncommon sense: *Trust yourself.* Through your ongoing connection to the source and to the psychic inside you, all awareness *is* flowing to you right now through every situation you encounter. And each one presents a precious chance to grow, to know, and to truly experience contentment with the flow of your life.

You've embarked on a wonderful journey. You'll encounter many interesting developments as you follow the path of your evolving uncommon sense. I'd love to hear all about them—whether it's in the form of sharing your uncommon sense discoveries, your questions, or certainly your responses to this book. Write to me! Yours in love and loads of uncommon sense,

Patricia Einstein

UNCOMMON TRICKS: FROM FINDING LOST OBJECTS TO CREATING UNCOMMON LOVE—AND MORE

FINDING LOST OBJECTS

First, take some deep breaths to relax into the receptive state that will help you get the information you need. Anxiety definitely chokes up the flow. When you're ready, put up your inner white screen. Then visualize the missing object all alone on the screen.

Now slowly widen your mental focus, gradually zooming your awareness out like a camera to bring the area immediately around the object into this mental picture. Look for visual clues that might tell you where you are. For example, if your screen reveals the inside of a drawer, what other objects do you see in the picture that might tell you in which drawer the missing object will be found? You might even try asking your larger self, "Where am I?"

If you need still more clues, try zooming out a little wider until more of the surrounding area comes into view. Or try mentally flashing backward in time from the lost object as it sits alone on your white screen. Imagine going back to where the object was right before it was lost. Look around. What do you see? What does the scene tell you about where your lost object may be now? If you're missing a watch, what time does the watch say when you look at it?

If your first few attempts don't help you locate your object, try again a little later, perhaps when you're not trying so hard. Finding lost objects is a lot like trying to remember someone's name—it's the sort of thing that doesn't always come to you right away, but often pops up unexpectedly later on. So be on the lookout for brief mental images that come to you later in the day, particularly when you're going to bed or even right after you've just woken up.

My husband used this technique to great effect. He'd lost a watch, and was very upset, but then he started to visualize the watch on his white screen. He checked for clues of what could be surrounding the watch, and he started to sense that it was in a dark place with some objects near it. A few moments later he realized that those surrounding objects were paper clips and the dark place was a hidden portion of a bookshelf. He went to the shelf, and sure enough, there the watch was, hidden under some papers and lying right next to a pile of paper clips!

READING THE PSYCHIC BAROMETER

You've learned how to tune in to your larger self for ongoing guidance and information. For quick answers to yes or no questions, however, nothing beats trying one of the following.

THE PENDULUM

This technique is adapted from an ancient tried-and-true method. Use a pendant if you have one, or create your own by taking a three-to-six-inch piece of string and attaching a little ball of tinfoil to one end so there's enough weight to allow the string, when held, to swing.

Holding your weighted string or pendant in your hand so it can swing freely from three to six inches on its chain, think of the question you want to ask. Now address your pendulum as you would address your larger self (think of the pendulum as an uncommon sense middle person).

The first question to ask your pendulum is what kind of movement will indicate a yes answer. Now begin to breathe deeply and rhythmically, and wait for the pendulum to start moving by itself. It will! Note whether it moves around in a circle or back and forth. Next, follow the same procedure to ask which kind of movement will indicate no.

Now ask your question, making sure that it can be answered by a yes or no (see "Finding the Answers in the Questions," Chapter 5), allowing the pendulum to move freely on its own.

Note: If your pendulum seems to move in a dramatic fashion (i.e., if it moves very surely in an unusually wide circle, or arcs more dramatically than usual to the left and right), interpret it as a psychic exclamation point at the end of the answer that's been given you. Sometimes it really will seem like your pendulum is sending you a very loud message of "Oh yes yes yes!" or "Oh no no no!" And at other times it may seem as if your pendulum's not moving at all, or else is moving too subtly to register a definite answer. In these cases, try again later, or try the following technique.

THE SPLIT SCREEN

Visualize your inner white screen and divide it in half. It, too, will function as your uncommon sense middle person, so ask it which side of the screen will indicate a yes answer, and by default, a no. Your uncommon sense may register these yes and no answers on the screen in any number of ways. It may do so by way of a flashing light radiating from the appropriate side. Or perhaps the correct side will move toward you, or signal you in some totally unique way. It may not even be visual: You may hear or feel an answer via your screen, or have a sense of which side of the screen seems right. Whatever works is right for you.

Again, as in the pendulum exercise, ask yourself a question that can be answered with yes or no, and note which side of your white screen responds. Here, too, a more intensified response means a more emphatic answer.

You can use the split screen technique very quickly in practically any everyday situation. Use it to test your business options, creative ideas, intuitive judgments, and so on, especially when you have to make an immediate decision. When you have the luxury of more time, add this technique to your review and decision-making process to give your comprehension an uncommon boost.

DEVELOPING UNCOMMON SENSE WITH OTHERS: SUGGESTED WORKOUTS TO SHARE

One of the wonderful bonuses of developing your uncommon sense is being able to share the fun and benefits with friends, intimate partners, and even business colleagues. You can quickly teach others whatever mechanics the two of you or the group need to learn collectively.

You'll see mutual results in no time, and in the bargain you'll get to know each other and even yourself much better as a result of developing your uncommon sense together.

Following are the exercises that I've found to be the best for sharing, many culled and adapted from this book, as well as some new ones that are especially good for specific situations. The suggestions are divided into two categories: *groups* (which can include friends, office colleagues, team members, fellow musicians, students, you name it) and an *intimate partners* category.

The following suggestions are really meant to be just that. Since every group is as unique as every individual, use your common and uncommon sense to choose the most feasible techniques for the people you know and the most workable order in which to practice them. You may find you have a group of people who want to meet on a regular basis to "work out" their uncommon sense. Remember, you can also spontaneously whip out any exercise that seems to be appropriate whenever *any* working group or team is at an impasse to get the ideas and energy flowing again.

While you're at it, whoever you're working out with, don't forget to have fun!

GROUPS

SPOON BENDING (EXERCISE 13). This gets folks into the swing of things by discovering hidden abilities and developing more trust in the uncommon sense process itself, which helps open them to try more exercises afterward. Even the most literal-minded individuals (or *especially* the most literal minded) seem to thoroughly enjoy this one. As mentioned earlier in the book, at the office you can try bending letter openers, too.

SYNCH GAMES (EXERCISES 10 AND 11). Adapt these exercises to suit your needs. Suggestions: Try synching with elevator doors, tuning in to the colors that friends, colleagues, or clients will be wearing on a given day, what time people will arrive at the office or at a party, when traffic lights will change. Keep track among your group, and exchange experiences and insights. You can even try using psychic drilling cards with a partner or partners to help improve your hit percentage.

Don't forget here and in all other exercises to cue others to clue into their own personal synch signals (p. 36). Also take note of how your friends and colleagues begin to synch in with each other, such as wearing the same colors or saying things at the same time.

RELAXING/RELEASING. The very exercises that helped you to start to relax and open to uncommon sense will help a group do the same. Try practicing "Breath Charge" (Exercise 22), "Neck Rolls" (Exercise 23), or "Spine Straightening" (Exercise 24) together.

IMAGING PRACTICE. Almost everyone responds to imaging exercises, and they're perfect for groups. Try any of the mind's eye imaging exercises (31–33). Show your group how to talk out what they're receiving with "Talking Pictures" (Exercise 34) and how to develop X-ray vision with Exercise 35. You may also want to photocopy the Visual/Feeling Checklist (p. 108) and distribute it to everyone in the group so all have an easy reference guide.

STORYTELLING (EXERCISE 37) is fun to do in a group almost anytime there's someone around to tune in to, for example, a new colleague or boss, a new client, people on line or in a restaurant, and so on. Try going around in a circle to build on to other group members' stories. This will give you an even richer narrative with even more to build on as everyone's details and insights are tuned in to and developed by the entire team.

FINDING THE ANSWERS IN THE QUESTIONS (EXERCISES 38 AND 39). If you feel your group is ready for a more "advanced" tuning-in exercise, this is a good one to try.

PSYCHOMETRY (EXERCISE 40). This exercise is a great crowd pleaser. Try passing around a dish of different guests' jewelry at a party. The results will be surprisingly good. In other group situations, start out by practicing with each other's jewelry or other objects. Then try a group tune-in on metal items belonging to a boss, co-worker, or client (use papers if you can't get anything metal, or try photographs or any other item belonging to the subjects in question).

OTHER GROUP SUGGESTIONS:

- Demonstrate the split screen technique (from the "Reading the Psychic Barometer" described earlier), and get your group to tune in to questions of mutual interest. For instance, at the office, ask how certain projects will turn out, and when with friends, how certain issues concerning one particular friend will be resolved.

- If you're interested in developing group creativity and success, try "Wordspin" (Exercise 44), "Fractured Proverbs" (Exercise 45), or "Likenings" (Exercise 46).

- You can also have fun showing how to jump start the right brain by doing the alternative nostril technique in the "Breath Charge" exercise. Silly as it looks, people really enjoy this one. They get a regular charge out of it!

- For a change of pace, try a group experience with "Dream Problem Solving" (Exercise 48). Pick a single creative problem and send everyone home to literally sleep on it. At the next group meeting (preferably the next day), put together a composite picture from those remembered dreams and you'll get a picture with some interesting similarities and guidance. Use the Visual/Feeling Checklist for interpretation.

- Locating the Essence/Finding the Feeling (see Chapter 6) is a great morale and team spirit booster. Make sure to try both parts of the exercise. Believe it or not, the metropolitan staff of one of the nation's leading news services had great fun casting each other as pastries!

- Especially good for business situations is the "Free-Form Free-for-All" (Exercise 51). Try it with a colleague to right-brainstorm marketing plans, new ideas and solutions, and so on.

- At the office again, it's most helpful to try "The Empathy Connection" (Exercise 54) to increase your group's creative problem-solving ability when the well seems to run dry.

INTIMATE PARTNERS

For more intimate uncommon sense development, you can certainly adapt any of the exercises from the above suggested group workouts.

OTHER INTIMATE SUGGESTIONS:

- The synch games are especially good ones to try.

- Since you are probably already at least somewhat in synch with your intimate partner, start with *synch games*, but go further with the exercises. Synch with phone calls, words, even thoughts.

- Try "Psychometry" and "Finding the Answer in a Question."

- You'll find that answering each other's questions can sometimes be easier than answering your own. You'll also be pleasantly surprised to find that when you tune in to an intimate partner you gain the bonus of receiving insightful information about yourself as well.

- Also try using the *white screen technique* to tune in to your partner's present, and then his or her future. Once you've got a clear picture in place, add yourself to the scene. Where do you fit in? Is there a message for you as well as him or her?

- To stimulate your *mutual love flow,* here's a new exercise to share.

LOVE JUMPS. Place your left hand on your partner's heart. Have him or her do the same to yours. Take hold of each other's right hands, and breathe deeply and rhythmically, looking deeply into each other's eyes.

Whole focus in this position for as long as you can. Feel the flow of energy between the two of you. That very palpable current is the literal love flow. Contacting it in this way together will not only put you in touch with its powerful energy, it will also clear the way for greater love to flow between you both now and later on.

This is an especially good technique to practice after experiencing some kind of problem. It helps you both get back on the literal love track. It's got another wonderful function: At the proper place and time, it serves as an incomparable prelude to an evening of deep lovemaking!

USING YOUR UNCOMMON SENSE TO CREATE UNCOMMON LOVE

Believe it or not, while you've been opening your mind to uncommon sense, you've also been opening your heart to love—your abilities to sense it around you and attract it to you. That's one of the wonderful benefits of practicing the energy line-up as well as many of the other exercises in this book. Love, like intuition, creativity, and wealth, is a natural part of the infinite riches that are available to you every time you connect with the source.

Using any of the following suggestions will help further strengthen your connection to your "love account," helping you to sense and expand the love in your life. You'll find they work almost like magic, whether you need to feel a general lift or want to work on some special love problem or situation. To really tap into love's mother lode, try the following exercise first.

MAKING YOUR LOVE CONNECTION

Warm up, and follow the energy-balancing exercise. When you're ready, bring your awareness back to your heart area. Now see a lovingly warm, pink light start to radiate from your heart energy center. Really breathe into that pink light and feel it grow. Experience it as a shining pink cloud of pure love.

When it's strong and bright, circulate the cloud of pink light throughout your entire body, warming each and every cell of your being with its loving glow. Bathe yourself in that light.

Now return the pink light back to your heart area, and then send it outward to the universe, affirming, "I now connect with the never-ending flow of infinite love." Feel and see the pink light saturate the entire universe with your love (by the way, this is the living embodiment of the expression "seeing the world through rose-colored glasses"). Now draw that light back to your heart, even pinker and warmer for its journey.

Once more, circulate the warm pink light throughout your whole body, and then bring it back to your heart area to roost. Really let yourself experience the glorious, pink love energy washing over and through you until you seem to merge together and become one with it.

OTHER LOVE SUGGESTIONS:

- Sometimes you need the *extra boost* of consciously releasing any feelings or situations that are not at all loving in your life. When you find yourself in this boat, first visualize any unloving or unloved feelings as a gray cloud hovering over your heart. Then, see the gray cloud being gently blown away, and replaced by a loving, billowing pink cloud. See that shining pink cloud envelop first your heart and then your entire being. Hold the vision and the affirmation as long as you want to. It feels great! Follow up with the previous making-your-love-connection exercise, if you'd like, for added emphasis.

- To help uncommonly *transform both relationships and situations through love,* try seeing that loving pink cloud enveloping both your self and your situation, whether it's a relationship, job, or home, and allowing it to lovingly permeate and bring a rosy sense of ease to all concerned.

- To *keep the love flowing in your life* make a point of consciously radiating pink light, whenever you think of it. Either concentrate on sending it glowing in all directions, or directly to anyone you'd like to send loving thoughts to. You'll start noticing a marked difference in both the way you generally feel—more naturally loving—and in the more naturally loving quality of the relationships surrounding you.

- For *better understanding and improving relationships* themselves, do your energy balancing, then make your love connections as outlined. Let your impressions flow, mentally talking out any impressions you receive and using the Visual/Feeling

Checklist to make sure you're getting all the information your impressions contain.

- If there is a *need for harmony* in the relationship (for example, problems with your employer/employee, a parent, or a child), try visualizing the two of you at either end of a gigantic golden scale. Then see the two of you finding the balance together, surrounded by golden light. Repeat this process whenever you feel the need.

- If you're still *looking for that perfect mate,* here's a trick that's worked for me, and one that's just too good to pass up: Try looking at your perfect mate as someone who's already very much part of your life, but just "away" for a while. In the sense that love is ever present, it certainly makes sense.

- And for *connecting with your perfect mate,* warm up, follow the energy-balancing exercise, and then make your love connection (following the first suggestion in this section). After you return the pink light to your heart from the universe, affirm, "I now open myself to my perfect mate. I know he (or she) will be here as I open to him (or her), and will appear as I need, when I am truly ready." Then, let your affirmation go, truly accepting that your mate will, indeed, come.

• • •

PLAYING THE BINGO LIST (UNCOMMON LOVE-STYLE)

Once loving prospects do start showing up, you'll want to use your uncommon sense to determine their rightness for you. When tuning in to a new love potential or relationship for that "bingo" sense of rightness, right from the start pay special attention to the following signals:

- *Feelings.* Remember to essentially "feel out" the person in question. It may seem obvious, but some people look so good on paper—and in person—you may ignore some basic negative uncommon sense feelings you have about them. This works the other way around, too, of course.

   Do follow up on any negative feelings you may have. As in some of the greatest romantic comedies, initial tensions can eventually lead to true romance. So, keep tuning in to see what other feelings and images come up until you reach a sense of potential resolution.

- *Images.* Try putting your new love interest on your white screen just as you've learned to do when checking out creative/business options. Does his or her image seem to stay on the screen, or does it fade away or flicker in and out? Is it richly detailed, or barely filled in? Do any personal symbols or images come up that tell you something? If you are tuning in to several different potential interests, which seems to have more life, more future?

Put yourself into the picture with the person in question and try the same techniques. Does that double image fare as described here or does it change? Try flashing forward. What are the two of you doing together? And, in all cases, what is the general feeling of the image or scene?

- *Synchronicity.* Check the flow of the relationship the way you do when you're checking out the rightness of ideas, jobs, or projects. Are things falling into place? Flowing? Do you just happen to run into him or her on a crowded city street—one where you usually never find yourself? Are there very interesting, very personal patterns that relate this person to the flow of all your love relationships, or do you intuit a sense of evolution from past relationships to this one? Is there a sense of harmony or attunement between the two of you? Do you find yourself saying the same things at the same time, or seem to immediately sense what the other is saying or thinking?

Note: Remember, don't analyze while you're in this whole checking-in process, because a lot of what you discover won't make logical sense. Love, like uncommon sense after all, is a nonrational phenomenon. But if you find, by following the list, that many experiences do indeed check out, bingo!

LIFE TRANSITION ROUTINE

This book has been full of suggestions for uncommonly developing many different areas of your life. But you may feel you need an extra development boost when you're going through a major life transition. This could include moments when you're experiencing an intense change or shift in jobs or careers, relationships, creative, spiritual or educational development, or at any time you find yourself involved in deep self-questioning.

For those periods, make sure you're *whole focusing* at least five minutes a day—thirty minutes would be great —to help break through any blocks you may be experiencing. To that end, pay special attention to your breathing. As well as spending a few moments a day doing *deep breathing* exercises, take deep uncommon sense breaths throughout the day, whenever you think of it.

Energy balancing (Exercise 17) is also especially important at these times. When you do this exercise, after you go through the energy lineup, try putting extra focus on the center and corresponding color that relate most closely to the issues you're dealing with. You can give yourself an *extra shot of color energy* by wearing the color in question, or keeping it around in plain view. For example, try using red flowers to help you focus on vitality or a blue scarf to help you focus on greater communication and creativity.

Do keep tuning in to your *white screen* for a clearer

picture of what's ahead, as well as for guidance through your present situation.

Pay special attention to the *feelings and images* that come to you at this time in your life—either through your white screen and other tuning-in exercises, or just at any moment in your everyday life. So, too, make note of especially *synchronistic* events happening, or interesting coincidences. They could provide a vital clue to a new direction you should take, or confirmation of a decision you've made or are in the process of making.

Keep noting these experiences in your *uncommon sense log,* and make sure to include any other interesting information you may be receiving, especially information from your dreams. Don't worry about all of it making sense. Your answers and direction will become clearer and clearer to you as you keep clearing your own path to uncommon sense.

SETTING UP YOUR UNCOMMON SENSE LOG

I strongly encourage you to set up your own uncommon sense log and to keep it handy when you try techniques and exercises. A really good place to keep the log when it's not in use is on your night table, so you can jot down those dreams and flashes of inspiration in the morning before they flow back to the source.

You can use any of the following for your uncommon sense log:

- black and white composition book
- a diary (with or without lock)
- looseleaf notebook
- accounting ledger with double columns
- steno pad
- spiral notebook of any size (the little ones with the spiral on top are good to carry around)
- index cards with a rubber band around them
- shoebox filled with slips of paper
- your personal computer and favorite word processing program
- a combination of any of the above, or whatever works for you!

If you like to dictate into a tape recorder, it's still probably a good idea to keep a written log around. This is because one of the great uses of an uncommon sense log is being able to flip through it quickly to pick up patterns in symbols and images as you begin to work up your own uncommon sense language. For most people, it's simply much easier and quicker to review pages than it is to review audio tapes. Certainly, continue taping your notes. But you might try to get into the habit of jotting down key images or insights in a small notebook—or even on the bottom line of your appointment book—as you record. Using the two methods together may even jog more insight.

WHAT AND WHEN TO WRITE IN YOUR UNCOMMON SENSE LOG

It doesn't matter how often you write in your log, as long as it feels right to you. Once a day, once a week, or once a month may be the perfect rhythm for you to collect your insights and spark more. Or you may find yourself writing feverishly every day for a few weeks or so and then not even thinking about it for a few weeks more. Writing in your log has its own special rhythm, just like developing your uncommon sense. Sometimes the two intersect, and sometimes they don't.

It is a good idea, however, to date your entries. When you look back later, this will give you important information about how your insights developed in relationship with events in your life—which in turn will give you more insight about how to pinpoint the information your uncommon sense has been giving you.

Use your log to jot down information about all your ongoing uncommon sense experiences. The discoveries you make with whole focusing, uncommon sense exercises alone or in a group, synchronicity, dreams, creativity, success, and sessions with a professional psychic advisor are all rich veins of uncommon sense experiences for you to record.

Start out by recording all of them, whenever you feel the need. Over time, you may find you're especially interested in writing about your dreams or about the experiences you have with psychometry, finding the answers in the questions, or other uncommon experiences you've had helping others. Or you may find you have a lot to say about how your uncommon sense comes through for you in your daily life. This is fine, too: Writing in your uncommon sense log is all about fine-tuning your own unique uncommon sense talents and needs.

It's also a good idea to review your entries every once in a while to see what pops up for you, and to write down your observations about patterns that come up, perhaps in a separate part of your log. (See the Patterns Checklist at the end of this Appendix.)

YOUR CREATIVITY LOG

In Chapter 6 we discussed logging creative experiences. If you've already started a creativity log, you can combine your uncommon sense log with your creativity log or run them separately. It's up to you. Some people find their intuitive experiences and creative ideas are so closely linked that each sparks the other. Others prefer the uncluttered feeling and enhanced focus that running two journals gives them. If you do opt to do them separately, try comparing them from time to time (maybe when you're doing your periodic review) to see what new creative ideas and personal insights are revealed.

PATTERNS CHECKLIST

- *Key words* or phrases in your entries

- *Recurring images* on your white screen

- *Colors* that keep coming up on your white screen, in your dreams, or during whole focusing (check Chapter 3 for interpretations, or use your own)

- *Feelings* or even physical sensations (chills, warmth, etc.) that come up during whole focusing or uncommon sense exercises

- *Signals* that may be your personal forms of confirmation (literal physical sensations or a more general gut feeling, a sense of absolute conviction, examples of synchronicity. These can change from time to time.)

- *Peak experiences* in your uncommon sense exercises (to pinpoint your special talents)

Note: Even if you don't think you're going to find any patterns, check for them anyway. As you focus on reviewing your log, your right brain can suddenly tick out associations between experiences you'd forgotten, or connections you've overlooked. And if you don't find any patterns, don't be surprised if one so clear you can't believe it escaped your attention percolates up later on in the day. When it does come up, don't forget to write it down. Finally, consider photocopying copies of the Visual/Feeling Checklist and the Patterns Checklist to staple inside the cover of your journal for quick reference. Or make up your own!

ABOUT THE AUTHOR

PATRICIA EINSTEIN is a successful New York psychic with an active practice that includes consultations, workshops, classes and lectures for private and corporate clients alike. Nicknamed the "Sensible Psychic," Einstein has the honor of being the only psychic ever listed in any Gault/Millau guide. Gault/Millau's *The Best of New York* praises her "uncanny accuracy" and unique "holistic approach." She studied her craft with some of the leading lights of the psychic community, and her client list includes celebrities and major corporations spanning the fields of politics, the law, publishing, the arts, advertising, Wall Street, design, and all the healing professions. She currently lives in New York City with her husband, Peter.